We the People:

Exploring the U.S. Constitution

Written by Charlotte S. Jaffe and Barbara T. Roberts
Illustrated by Karen Neulinger and James Uttel

Educational Impressions™

ISBN 1-56644-968-5 (10-digit)
978-1-56644-968-7 (13-digit)

© 1987 Educational Impressions, Inc., Hawthorne, NJ
Second Edition © 1994 Educational Impressions, Inc.
Third Edition © 2007 Educational Impressions, Inc.

EDUCATIONAL IMPRESSIONS, INC.
Hawthorne, NJ 07507

Printed in the United States of America.

Table of Contents

To the Teacher

We the People provides a comprehensive look at the people and issues involved in the formation of the Constitution. In addition to the factual story of the creation of the document there are included in the resource a variety of materials to encourage critical and creative thinking, vocabulary games and puzzles, and an intriguing trivia section. There is also a Mock Convention Section that presents guidelines for the development of a simulated classroom Constitutional Convention. A quiz, which may be given as a pre- or post-test, is also included.

SECTION I: The Story of the Constitution

The objective of this section is to familiarize students with the main events and issues associated with the development of the Constitution: the weaknesses of the Articles of Confederation, the Northwest Ordinance, the Annapolis Convention, convention compromises, the importance of the Bill of Rights, federal vs. state powers, checks and balances, and the separation of powers. The constitutional trivia information may also be used as the basis for a classroom trivia game.

SECTION II: Profiles of the Framers of the Constitution

This section contains the biographies of the most important and colorful delegates to the Constitutional Convention. Seventy-four men were named as delegates; fifty-five of them attended the Convention and thirty-nine were signers. Students may use the profile information to complete activities in the Critical- and Creative-Thinking Section and in the Mock Convention Section.

SECTION III: Vocabulary Activities

Students are asked to find definitions for a given vocabulary list. A variety of activities reinforce comprehension and usage.

Answers to Word Shapes

1. veto	6. federal	11. republic
2. tranquility	7. ratify	12. legislative
3. delegates	8. convention	13. Supreme Court
4. judicial	9. representative	14. unanimously
5. amend	10. articles	15. compromise

Answers to Scrambled Words

1. unconstitutional	6. tranquility	11. amendment
2. preamble	7. amend	12. federal
3. representative	8. framework	13. ratify
4. legislative	9. republic	14. veto (or vote)
5. convention	10. articles	

Answers to Match-ups

1. B	3. G	5. E	7. C	9. K	11. H
2. D	4. L	6. F	8. J	10. A	12. I

Answers to True or False

1. F	4. T	7. T	10. F	13. T
2. F	5. T	8. F	11. F	14. T
3. T	6. T	9. F	12. F	15. F

SECTION IV: Critical- and Creative-Thinking Activities

A variety of activities to challenge students' critical- and creative-thinking abilities is offered. Choose all or some.

Answers to Fact or Opinion

1. F	4. F	7. O	10. F	13. F
2. O	5. F	8. F	11. F	14. F
3. O	6. F	9. O	12. O	

Answers to Putting the Constitution to Work

1. E   2. L   3. J   4. L   5. J

Answers to Let's Debate!

Question No. 1 was settled by having one President whose powers were checked by the other two branches of government. Question No. 2 was settled by the Great Compromise, which called for equal representation in the Senate and proportional representation in the House of Represenatives. Question No. 3 was settled by giving the federal government authority over those matters of common concern to the people of all the states and by enumerating those powers delegated to the federal government; powers not specifically granted to the federal government, nor denied to the states, were retained by the states.

Answers to Systems Check

Congress Checks the President: The House of Representatives can impeach (accuse of unlawful acts) the President if he or she is thought to be guilty of "treason, bribery, or high crimes and misdemeanors." The President would then be tried by the Senate and if found guilty, removed from office. Although a President can make a treaty, it must be approved by a two-thirds vote of the Senate to be ratified. The Senate must confirm the appointment of cabinet and other important officials. Congress has control of taxes and expenditures and can interfere with policies requiring money. Also, Congress can override a presidential veto with a two-thirds vote.

Congress Checks the Supreme Court: Congress has the power to impeach federal judges. Congress determines the number of justices on the Supreme Court. Congress must approve the appointment of federal judges.

The President Checks the Supreme Court: The President appoints federal judges and can appoint people sympathetic to his views on important issues. The President has the power to grant pardons and reprieves to people who have been convicted in the federal courts.

The President Checks Congress: The President has the power to veto legislation passed by Congress. The President can call a special session to ask for the passage of a specific law.

The Supreme Court Checks the President: The Supreme Court can declare a law approved by the President to be unconstitutional.

The Supreme Court Checks the President: The Supreme Court can declare a law passed by Congress to be unconstitutional.

Answers to Time Line

A. 5   B. 4   C. 3   D. 7   E. 2   F. 10   G. 1   H. 8   I. 6   J. 9

SECTION V: Mock Convention

Re-create the Constitutional Convention in your classroom. Begin by choosing a student to play the role of George Washington, president of the convention. The other students then each select a delegate to portray. Encourage the students to research the delegate in depth. Some of the activities require additional research by the students. It is important that the students accumulate sufficient background information before proceeding with the simulation. The Rules of Procedure page provides guidelines for conducting the convention. With the class, decide on which issues to simulate in the classroom. A study of Independence Hall may enhance the students' background knowledge.

RESOURCES

Additional reference materials are included: a quiz to be used before and/or after presenting the unit, a list of delegates and ratification dates, and a suggested list of reading materials.

Answers to Quiz

1. The Bill of Rights
2. James Madison
3. They feared a repeat of the tyranny of the King of England.
4. Some of the weaknesses were as follows: the lack of the power to control foreign and interstate
5. trade, the lack of valid useful money, the lack of the power to tax, the lack of the power to control the army and the navy, and the lack of power to enforce treaties.
6. Preamble
7. Connecticut
8. It keeps any one branch from becoming too powerful.
9. Northwest Ordinance
10. Rhode Island
11. Delaware
12. *Federalist*

13. H	14. G	15. F	16. C	17. A	18. B	19. D	20. E

SECTION I:
The Story of the Constitution

On the following pages you will read the story of the creation of one of the most famous documents in history: the Constitution of the United States of America. Who were the men who conceived it? Why was it developed? What guidelines does it contain? What elements have kept it so successful for so many years? You will find the answers to these and other thoughtful questions as you follow the remarkable tale of the growth of the Constitution. All American citizens are greatly indebted to the learned leaders of 1787 who wrote this unique document.

The Articles of Confederation

After the Americans declared their independence from Great Britain, they realized that there was a great need for a plan of government that would unite the states. On June 11, 1776, the Continental Congress appointed a committee to devise a workable plan of unity. One month later the committee, headed by John Dickinson of Delaware, had written such a plan. It was called the Articles of Confederation. The word *confederation* means association, and the new document called for a "firm league of friendship" among the states.

Although the Articles of Confederation were adopted by the delegates in 1777, they were not ratified by all the states until 1781. Some states approved them quickly, but others debated the provisions for years. Maryland was the last state to ratify the Articles. In March 1781 the plan was finally approved as the first constitution for the new nation.

Under the Articles of Confederation, the Congress had few powers. People were afraid to develop another strong central government. They had been opposed to the strong power of the King of England and they did not want that situation repeated in their new government. They decided to give most of the power to the individual states. Each state was given one vote in Congress, and nine votes were needed to pass a law. Any amendment to the Articles would need the approval of all thirteen states. These rulings made agreement on any proposed law quite difficult to obtain.

One law that did manage to gain approval of the Congress of the Confederation was the Northwest Ordinance of 1787. This law gave Congress the right to govern territorial lands. It offered guidelines to help the settlers turn their lands into states. Thomas Jefferson was the author of the Northwest Ordinance. Some of its provisions are still being used today. The Northwest Territory was later divided into five states: Michigan, Wisconsin, Indiana, Illinois, and Ohio.

Although the Northwest Ordinance was a fine achievement, the Articles of Confederation also had many weaknesses. One major problem centered around money. Although Congress had the power to ask the states for money, it could not tax them. Because most of the states refused to contribute money, the government was usually in need. Soldiers did not receive their wages, and war debts could not be repaid. Also, each state printed its own currency; therefore, the values varied from state to state. The same coin could be worth 75 cents in New York and 50 cents in Virginia. Paper money called Continental currency was printed, but it had neither gold nor silver to back it and was, therefore, virtually worthless.

Under the Articles of Confederation, Congress had no power to control trade between states or between states and a foreign country. Each state passed its own set of commerce laws according to its own economic interests. Because colonial roads were poorly developed, travel was difficult. Most colonists did not often venture beyond their own state boundaries. They regarded themselves as Virginians or Pennsylvanians rather than as citizens of the United States.

Another problem concerned the armed forces. Congress did not have its own army or navy; therefore, it had to rely on the individual states to supply troops in an emergency. In 1786 Daniel Shays, a Revolutionary War soldier, led a group of one thousand disgruntled Massachusetts farmers in an attempt to seize a local courthouse. The men were protesting the seizure of their farms because of debts. The national government could not stop the uprising, and the Massachusetts troops were called in to end the rebellion.

Throughout the states, many citizens became concerned about the weakness of the national government. Under the Articles of Confederation, Congress could not seem to control quarrels that arose between states. Thoughtful leaders, such as George Washington, realized that something had to be done to hold the union together.

The Constitutional Convention

In September 1776 delegates from each of the states were asked to attend a meeting in Annapolis, Maryland. The topic of discussion was to be a uniform system of trade regulations; however, delegates from only five states attended: New Jersey, New York, Pennsylvania, Delaware, and Virginia. Little could be accomplished. Alexander Hamilton, the delegate from New York, suggested still another meeting time and place, not only to discuss trade regulations, but also to discuss the weaknesses of the Articles of Confederation. He felt that if invitations to the next meeting came from Congress, more states would send representatives. The other delegates agreed to meet in May 1787 and to set Philadelphia as the location for the convention.

Colonial Philadelphia was a colorful and cosmopolitan city. Horse-drawn carriages rumbled through the narrow cobblestone streets. Throughout the waterfront, marketplace merchants could be heard loudly hawking their wares. The delgates did not all arrive on time for the first meeting day. Travel was slow and difficult. It took two weeks to journey from New Hampshire and almost three weeks from Georgia. The roads around Philadelphia were deep in mud from almost a week's steady rainfall. Finally, fifty-five representatives from twelve states gathered at Independence Hall, which was also the Pennsylvania State House, to begin the work of revising the Articles of Confederation. Only the state of Rhode Island did not send a delegate. The delegates soon decided that the best way to solve the problems would be to create a new constitutional plan for their government.

Once the rules were established, the first order of business was to elect a president of the convention. Tall, dignified and well-respected, George Washington was unanimously chosen to be the leader. The delegates sat at tables covered in green baize (imitation felt), in the same room where the Declaration of Independence had been signed. The high windows were covered with slatted blinds to keep out the hot sun. Sand was spread on nearby cobblestone streets to quiet the noise of wagon wheels. The delegates agreed to keep secret all the proceedings of the meetings until the end of the convention.

Most of the delegates were politically experienced, well-educated and gifted writers or orators. The majority had received law degrees, and many had served in the Revolutionary War and in the Continental Congress. Benjamin Franklin at eighty-one years of age was the oldest delegate and was called the "peacemaker" of the convention. He often added just the right words to ease a disagreement and to encourage compromise. James Madison from Virginia kept a journal of the proceedings of each meeting. Because of his many valuable contributions, Madison is often called the "Father of the Constitution." Alexander Hamilton of New York was a strong supporter of a powerful federal government and was very influential during the proceedings. Thomas Jefferson and John Adams were both serving as foreign ministers and did not attend the convention.

Representation

One of the main sources of conflict was the disagreement between the large and small states over the way they would be represented in Congress. Edmund Randolph of Virginia presented the Virginia Plan. According to this plan, the Congress was to be divided into two houses. In the first house, the members would be elected according to the population of the state. The members of the first house would elect the members of the second house. Small states opposed this plan; they feared they would have little say in government affairs. Other states felt that the federal government would become too powerful. William Paterson, a delegate from New Jersey, introduced the New Jersey Plan. This plan provided for equal representation in Congress, regardless of population. Under this plan, small states would remain strong, but the plan did not guarantee direct representation.

The two plans were strongly debated. Roger Sherman, a Connecticut delegate, finally proposed a compromise plan. This plan is called the Great Compromise; it is also known as the Connecticut Compromise. According to the Great Compromise, Congress would have two houses: the Senate and the House of Representatives. The number of members representing each state in the House was to be determined by the population of the state. In the Senate each state would be given equal representation: two senators and two votes. Because all laws needed the approval of both the House and the Senate to pass, the small states felt that this compromise was fair and that it sufficiently protected them; they agreed to vote for it.

Presidential Election

Another major question concerned the election of the President. James Wilson of Pennsylvania proposed that the chief executive be chosen by electors who would represent different state districts. Some delegates thought that the national legislatures should choose the President and some others wondered if there should be more than one person to do such a very important job. The President's election and qualifications were heavily debated throughout the convention. It was finally decided that the President should be elected by electors chosen by the states and should be at least thirty-five years old and a citizen of the United States.

The Slavery Question

The question of whether slaves should be counted in the general population census was one that caused great disagreement. Most southern representatives wanted the slaves to be counted but did not want to pay taxes for them. Most northern states did not want the slaves counted because it would give the South a population advantage in the House of Representatives; however, they did want them counted for taxation purposes. The delegates reached a compromise that would allow three-fifths of the the slaves to be counted for both population and taxation.

The Trade Decision

How should Congress regulate trade? This problem was also settled by a compromise. Southern states opposed regulations that would curtail the slave trade. Also, the South was engaged in exporting most of its goods to foreign countries and did not want high duties. Northern states favored more regulations over foreign trade by Congress. They wanted higher import duties placed on goods and materials coming from foreign nations, for they were developing manufacturing industries of their own. The compromise they worked out did give Congress the right to regulate trade, but it could not limit the slave trade for twenty years, nor would there be any export tax levied.

Completion of the Constitution

Before the work of the Constitutional Convention was completed, the delegates decided on a system of amendments that would allow the Constitution to continue to grow in order to meet the changing times. Gouverneur Morris of Pennsylvania was selected to write the words of the completed document in its final form.

The final session of the Constitutional Convention was held on September 17, 1787. The delegates were proud of the work that they had accomplished during the long, hot summer. Because Benjamin Franklin was out of the country, James Wilson read the speech that Franklin had prepared. In it, he urged swift adoption of the Constitution. Thirty-nine delegates signed the document before they left Philadelphia. Each state planned to hold a convention within its borders to vote on the adoption of the Constitution. Ratification by nine states was needed to make the Constitution effective.

The Constitution is Approved

On December 7, 1787, Delaware became the first state to ratify the Constitution. Pennsylvania, New Jersey, Connecticut and Georgia also approved it within a few months; however, the path to final adoption was not an easy one. Two opposing groups emerged: those who supported the Constitution were called Federalists; those who were against its adoption were called Anti-Federalists. Alexander Hamilton of New York, along with John Jay, wrote a series of essays in which they clearly argued for passage of the Constitution. Those essays were printed in newspapers and later published under the title *The Federalist.* These Federalist Papers did a great deal to muster support! In Virginia another raging battle was taking place between the Federalists and the Anti-Federalists. Patrick Henry spoke vehemently against the Constitution, fearing the President might turn into a royal monarch.

In the final vote taken on June 25, 1788, however, Virginia voted 89-79 in favor of ratification. When the Federalists in New York heard about Virginia's approval of the Constitution, they knew that their cause would soon be won. Upon hearing the news of Virginia's approval and not wanting to become isolated, the New York Convention immediately voted to ratify it by a count of 30-27. The Constitution was now law! Nine states had ratified it. Congress could now begin the process of governing under the new document. The electors unanimously elected George Washington to be the first President of the United States; they chose John Adams to be Vice-President.

The Bill of Rights

The first ten amendments to the Constitution are known collectively as the Bill of Rights; they were added to the document in 1791. These amendments were based upon ideas already in many of the state constitutions. Many delegates signed the Constitution with the understanding that a bill of rights would be added at the first session of Congress! The amendments protect individuals from government; however, neither the freedoms nor the rights are unlimited, and all have certain conditions.

Summary of the Bill of Rights

Amendment 1: FREEDOM OF RELIGION, SPEECH, PRESS, ASSEMBLY AND PETITION
This amendment guarantees that citizens can practice their own religion. It also gives freedom of the press and freedom of speech.

Amendment 2: RIGHT TO KEEP ARMS
This gives citizens the right to bear arms (own weapons) for "lawful" reasons.

Amendment 3: QUARTERING OF TROOPS
In times of peace, citizens cannot be forced to have soldiers living in their homes. Even in times of war it can only be done as set forth in law.

Amendment 4: SEARCH AND SEIZURE—WARRANTS
This protects the citizens against unreasonable searches of their persons, homes, and property. The government must follow a certain set of rules to get permission to make a search.

Amendment 5: RIGHTS OF ACCUSED PERSONS
One cannot be tried for the same crime twice, nor can one be forced to act as witness against oneself. One's property cannot be taken without "due process" of the law.

Amendment 6: RIGHT TO SPEEDY TRIAL
This amendment gives the accused person the right to a speedy and public trial by an impartial jury and the right to have assistance of counsel in his/her defense.

Amendment 7: JURY TRIAL IN CIVIL CASES
This gives people the right to a jury trial in suits involving property valued above $20.00. Because there are many other laws covering such controversies, this amendment is seldom used.

Amendment 8: BAIL, FINES, AND PUNISHMENT
This protects citizens from excessive bail or fines. This also guarantees the freedom from cruel and unusual punishments. (These are usually defined by the Supreme Court.)

Amendment 9: POWERS RESERVED TO THE PEOPLE
This amendment says that if a right is not specifically listed in the Constitution, it does not mean that the right is denied to the people.

Amendment 10: POWERS RESERVED TO THE STATES
The powers not delegated to the United States by the Constitution, nor prohibited by the Constitution to the states, are reserved to the states or to the people.

These ten amendments are considered by many to be the foundation of Americans' individual freedom!

Federal vs. State Powers

The delegates at the Constitutional Convention had much experience with different forms of government. They knew, therefore, that the government being formed must be strong in order to work. They also knew, from experience, that the strength must somehow be controlled, or "held in check" from becoming too powerful.

It was agreed that the central government would have the power to control things that involved all the states:

1. The federal government would have the right to make laws to exercise its powers.

2. The federal government, not the states, would decide to declare war, sign treaties or organize armies.

3. The federal government would establish relations with foreign countries.

4. The federal government would oversee interstate business and trade.

5. Only the central government would decide upon the system of money and its value throughout the nation.

6. The federal government would keep the right to tax people.

7. The federal government would organize the system of courts, deciding questions about the Constitution and settling questions between the states.

At the same time, each state would keep the powers to control all the matters within its own boundaries. Those powers not specifically given to the federal government would automatically become powers of the states and the people.

Avoiding Tyranny
Separating the Powers

To guard against the possibility of federal powers becoming misused by a single individual or group, the "Founding Fathers" wisely chose to separate the powers given to the federal government. They designed a federal government made up of three sections, or branches: the legislative, the executive, and the judicial. Each of the branches would have its own specific responsibilities and authority.

The legislative branch, or Congress, creates the laws. It is further divided into the House of Representatives and the Senate. Each state sends two representatives to the Senate. The number of representatives each sends to the House of Representatives depends upon the population of the state. A law must pass both houses of Congress in order to become official.

The executive branch sees to it that the laws are put into effect and that they are obeyed. The President is the Chief Executive.

The judicial branch includes the Supreme Court and other federal courts. It is the responsibility of this branch of the government to interpret the laws. This branch is also responsible for deciding cases in which federal laws are in question and for settling disputes between states.

Checks and Balances

In addition to the separation of federal powers into branches, the delegates decided upon a system of Checks and Balances. They believed this would prevent any one branch from becoming too powerful. The powers of each of the three branches are limited in some important ways by the other two branches.

Congress's power to pass laws can be limited by both the President and the Supreme Court. The President may veto a law if he (or she!) believes it to be unwise. Of course, Congress can overcome the veto, but only with at least a two-thirds vote. The Supreme Court has the power to declare a law unconstitutional.

Presidential powers are limited by Congress and by the Supreme Court. Although the President has the power to make treaties with foreign governments, Congress must approve those treaties before they become official. A bill approved by the President can be declared unconstitutional by the federal judiciary. Also, a President can be impeached, or accused of wrongdoing, by the House of Representatives and tried by the Senate. If found guilty, the President can be removed from office.

The powers of the judicial branch of government are also limited. Supreme Court justices and federal judges are named by the President and they must be approved by Congress. They, too, can be removed through the process of impeachment. The President can check the power of the judiciary through the power to grant pardons and reprieves.

The Constitutional Government of the United States

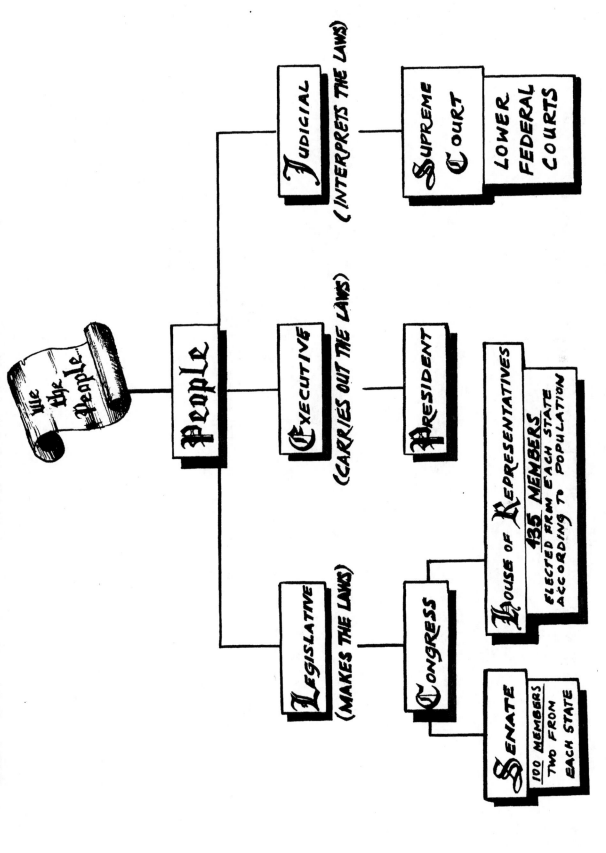

The System of Checks and Balances

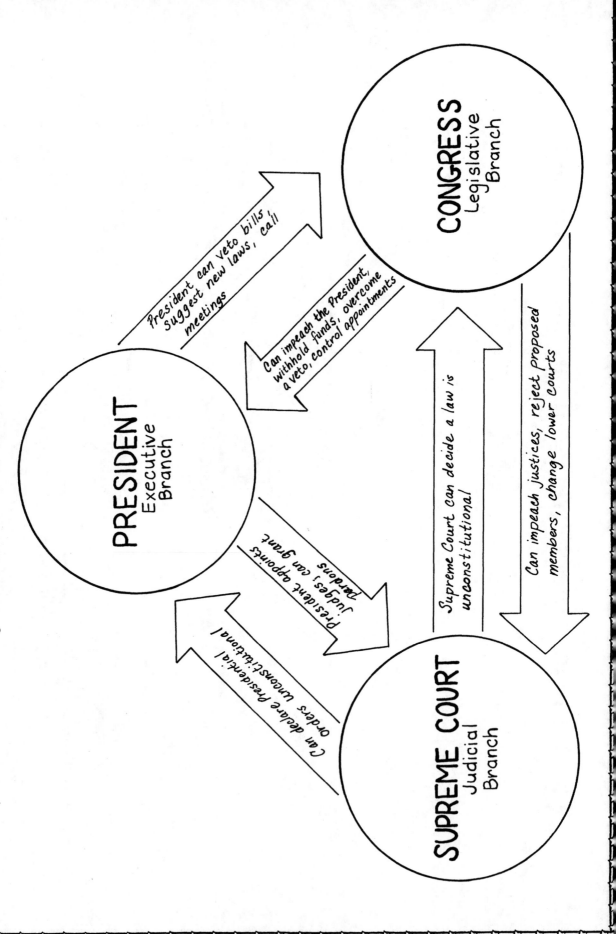

CONGRESS
Legislative Branch

PRESIDENT
Executive Branch

SUPREME COURT
Judicial Branch

President can veto bills, suggest new laws, call meetings

Can impeach the President, withhold funds, overcome a veto, control appointments

President appoints judges, can grant pardons

Can declare Presidential orders unconstitutional

Supreme Court can decide a law is unconstitutional

Can impeach justices, reject proposed members, change lower courts

Constitutional Amendments

One of the unique qualities of the United States Constitution is its ability to grow or change according to current needs. This is done through the system of amendments. As of now, twenty-six amendments have been added to the Constitution. The first ten are the Bill of Rights.

Susan B. Anthony led the fight for
adoption of the nineteenth amendment.

Nineteenth Amendment (Ratified in August 1920)

The right of citizens of the United States to vote shall not be denied or abridged by the United States, or by any State, on account of sex. Congress shall have the power, by appropriate legislation, to enforce the provisions of this article.

It was not until this amendment was passed in 1920 that American women were given the right to vote. Suffragette movements, groups of politically-minded women, had organized throughout the country in an effort to gain reform. Susan B. Anthony led the bitter and hostile fight for the adoption of the nineteenth amendment.

Twenty-second Amendment (Ratified in February 1951)

No person shall be elected to the office of the President more than twice, and no person who has held the office of President, or acted as President, for more than two years of a term to which some other person was elected President shall be elected to the office of the President more than once. But this article shall not apply to any person holding the office of President when this article was proposed by the Congress, and shall not prevent any person who may be holding the office of President, or acting as President, during the term within which this article becomes operative from holding the office of President or acting as President during the remainder of such term.

This amendment, which states that a President cannot be elected for more than two terms, was adopted as a result of the four-term presidency of Franklin D. Roosevelt. When Dwight Eisenhower was ending his second term in office, there was some support for repeal of the amendment; however, the effort was not sustained.

Twenty-sixth Amendment (Ratified in June 1971)

The right of citizens of the United States, who are eighteen years of age or older, to vote shall not be denied or abridged by the United States or any state on account of age.

Although Congress had changed the voting age from twenty-one years to eighteen years as part of the Voting Rights Act of 1970, this law applied only to voting in national elections. This amendment guaranteed eighteen-year-olds the right to vote in any election. It was ratified partly because of the increased political participation of young citizens during the late 1960's. The eighteen-year-olds proved that they were knowledgeable and sufficiently mature to assume the duties of responsible citizens.

Constitutional Trivia
Did You Know?

You may find the following facts of particular interest in your study of the development of the United States Constitution. You may use the statements as questions to ''test'' your family, friends, and classmates.

Delegates

The average age of the delegates was forty-three.

Jonathan Dayton from New Jersey was the youngest at twenty-six.

Benjamin Franklin of Pennsylvania was oldest at eighty-one.

Eight of the delegates had also signed the Declaration of Independence.

Seven of the delegates had been governors of their states.

Delegates came from every state except Rhode Island.

One-half of the delegates were lawyers.

Eight delegates were merchants and traders.

Five delegates were planters.

Three delegates practiced medicine.

Three of the delegates were office-holders.

There were one financier and one political scientist.

Twenty-four delegates had fought in the Revolutionary War.

One-half of the delegates owned slaves.

Seventy-nine men were named as delegates; fifty-five were sent to the meeting in Philadelphia.

George Washington

George Washington was one of the tallest men at the convention.

He admonished the delegates by telling them to be more careful about leaving papers lying around so that information wouldn't leak to the newspapers.

During the meetings he stayed at the home of Robert Morris.

Benjamin Franklin

Benjamin Franklin was known as the "Peacemaker of the Constitutional Convention."

It is said that during the proceedings Franklin had often wondered about a painting on the back of Washington's chair. It depicted the sun, but the artist had not made it clear whether it was a sunrise or a sunset. At the end of the convention, Franklin said that he felt sure it was symbolic of the new nation and that indeed it was a rising sun.

Benjamin Franklin made the motion that the Constitution be signed.

William Pierce described Franklin at the Constitutional Convention: "He is eighty-one years old but he possesses activity of mind equal to youth of twenty-five years of age."

Franklin told a story about a snake to Reverend Cutler of Massachusetts, who had come to visit in Philadelphia. He showed him a snake with two heads and said, "Wouldn't it be a shame if one head wanted to go one way and the other head in a different direction? The snake would go no place; it would just stay there until it died. That must not happen with the Constitutional Convention."

William Jackson

Jackson was chosen to be secretary of the convention.

James Madison

Madison became known as the "Father of the Constitution."

He was also known as the "Great Little Madison."

Madison later became the fourth President of the United States.

Gouverneur Morris

Gouverneur Morris was recorded as the most frequent speaker. The clear, concise language of the Constitution is largely a result of Morris's splendid command of the English language.

Charles Pinckney

Pinckney proposed the design for the Great Seal of the United States.

Roger Sherman

Roger Sherman was the only delegate who signed the Declaration of Independence, the Articles of Confederation, and the Constitution.

The Document

The American Bill of Rights was named after the British Bill of Rights, passed by Parliament in 1680.

It is the oldest functioning national constitution in the world.

It is displayed and protected in the National Archives in Washington, D.C.

The nickname of Connecticut is ''The Constitution State.''

Delaware was the first state to ratify the document.

The document was moved to Virginia when the British attacked the city of Washington, D.C., during the War of 1812.

The Constitution was written, printed, bound, and distributed to the delegates in less than five days.

The printing press was hand-inked and hand-operated.

Quotations

George Mason: ''The eyes of the United States are turned upon this assembly.''

Thomas Jefferson to John Adams: ''It is really an assembly of demi-gods.''

James Wilson originated the phrase ''the Federal Republic.''

Daniel Carroll, describing the Constitution: ''Anything nearer to perfection could not have been accomplished.''

Gouverneur Morris about the disagreement between the large and small states over the issue of representation: ''The fate of America was suspended by a hair.''

States Represented at the Constitutional Convention

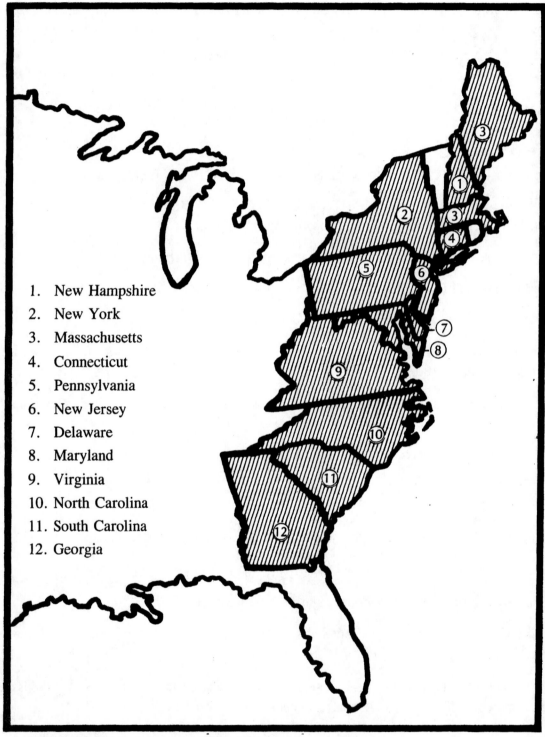

1. New Hampshire
2. New York
3. Massachusetts
4. Connecticut
5. Pennsylvania
6. New Jersey
7. Delaware
8. Maryland
9. Virginia
10. North Carolina
11. South Carolina
12. Georgia

NOTE: Rhode Island did not send any delegates.

SECTION II:
Profiles
of the
Framers of the
Constitution

Fifty-five delegates met in Philadelphia in May 1787 with the goal of revising or replacing the Articles of Confederation. The delegates to the Constitutional Convention were an outstanding group of men. They had been involved in the forging of the new nation and had continued to support it actively. They were deeply dedicated to this new responsibility facing them.

Of those gathered, the average age was forty-three. Most had participated in the Revolutionary War. Eight had signed the Declaration of Independence. More than half had been members of their state governments. Several had served as diplomats to European nations.

As it turned out, thirteen of the delegates were not present at the time the document was completed and ready to sign. A few left in protest. Some had to attend to pressing affairs at home. Of those that remained, three did not sign because they were not in total agreement with the final draft of the document.

DELAWARE

Delaware was the first state to ratify the Constitution.
(December 7, 1787)

Richard Bassett   Gunning Bedford, Jr.   Jacob Broom

John Dickinson   George Read

Richard Bassett

Richard Bassett was born in Cecil County, Maryland, in 1745. His father deserted the family and Richard was adopted by a relative. In 1776 he served on the state constitutional convention committee and was twice elected state senator. He attended the Annapolis Convention.

At the Constitutional Convention, Bassett voted against allowing a veto for the national congress on state laws deemed improper. He was one of the first U.S. senators from Delaware and was elected governor of the state in 1799. Two of his grandsons also served as senators.

Gunning Bedford, Jr.

Gunning Bedford, born in Philadelphia in 1747, was the fifth of eleven children. He attended the College of New Jersey, now called Princeton University, with James Madison and later studied law in the Philadelphia firm of Joseph Reed. His law practice was founded near Wilmington, Delaware. Bedford was a large man with a bold manner of speaking. His political views were generally conservative.

Bedford was an ardent supporter of the rights of small states at the Constitutional Convention. He favored limiting the powers of the federal government. He voted against the motion for proportional representation in the Senate. Bedford was also outspoken in favor of a three-year presidential term and a limitation placed on the number of re-elections.

George Read

John Dickinson

Gunning Bedford, Jr.

Richard Bassett

Jacob Broom

Jacob Broom was born in Wilmington, Delaware, in 1752. His first trade was that of a surveyor. He also worked in the real estate business and was the first postmaster of Wilmington. In 1784 he became a New Castle deputy in the State House of Representatives; he served two terms. Broom was also active in the cotton business in Delaware.

Broom was a quiet man with plain tastes. During the Constitutional Convention debates, he favored a nine-year term for senators. He also took part in the debates concerning the presidential term of office. His son and grandson also served in the state legislature.

John Dickinson

John Dickinson was born in Maryland in 1732, the son of wealthy parents. He and his family moved to Delaware in 1740. John was raised as a member of the Society of Friends. As a young boy, he received his education from a private tutor and later attended law school in London. After graduating, Dickinson married and established a thriving law practice in Philadelphia. Although he opposed the use of force to solve the conflict between England and the colonies, he did object to the unfair taxation by the king. He wrote a series of unsigned letters to the *Pennsylvania Chronicle* called "Letters from a Farmer." The letters criticized for the Townshend Acts of 1767. As a result, Dickinson was nicknamed "The Farmer."

Dickinson entered politics by serving in the Pennsylvania legislature. He often disagreed with Benjamin Franklin on political issues. He was a delegate to the Continental Congress but did not sign the Declaration of Independence. Dickinson was the author of the first draft of the Articles of Confederation. He later moved back to Delaware and became involved in state politics there. Dickinson attended the Constitutional Convention as a Delaware delegate in 1787. As a representative of a small state, he favored having one branch elected by the people and another modeled after the House of Lords in England.

George Read

George Read was born in Cecil County, Maryland, in 1734. His father, John Read, was the founder of the city of Charlestown, Maryland. George was one of six sons. When George was young, the family moved to New Castle, Delaware. He studied at a private academy in Pennsylvania and later attended law school in Philadelphia. When he returned to Delaware in 1754, he quickly established a law practice along with a small farm.

Read became state attorney general and served in the state assembly for twelve years. He married in 1763 and had four sons and one daughter. Read was elected to the Continental Congress, where he was a moderate who hoped for reconciliation with England.

Unlike other delegates from small states, at the Constitutional Convention Read favored a strong national government; however, he did fear the power of the large states and voted against proportional representation in the lower house of Congress. Read was described as an excellent judge and lawyer, but a tiresome public speaker.

PENNSYLVANIA

Pennsylvania was the second state to ratify the Constitution.
(December 12, 1787)

George Clymer	**Benjamin Franklin**	**Thomas Mifflin**
Gouverneur Morris	**Robert Morris**	**James Wilson**

Benjamin Franklin

Benjamin Franklin, affectionately called Dr. Franklin by his friends, was born in Boston, Massachusetts, in 1706. He was the fifteenth of seventeen children. Benjamin had various jobs beginning at age ten. At seventeen he was on his own. Very soon he was in the printing business in Philadelphia, publishing among other things *Poor Richard's Almanac.* He was responsible for founding the city's first volunteer fire department and America's first hospital. He also invented bifocals and the Franklin stove, investigated lightning as a source of electricity, and improved the postal system.

Franklin lived in England from 1766 to 1776. While there, he represented the colonies in opposition to the Stamp Act. He returned home and was a signer of the Declaration of Independence. Later he became minister to France and succeeded in persuading the French government to recognize the United States as an independent country and to help in its fight against the British.

Benjamin Franklin was the oldest delegate to the Constitutional Convention. He was a valuable member because of his experience in politics and government. His sense of humor and wisdom also proved invaluable. He was usually one to keep a discussion to the point, to identify the advantages and disadvantages of a proposal, and to cool tempers when necessary.

Franklin was out of the country at the end of the convention; therefore, James Wilson read for him the address Franklin had written to the delegates of the Constitutional Convention. In this message Franklin expressed the idea that the Constitution, although imperfect, was as close to perfect as was humanly possible. He put forth the motion that the work of the delegates be considered completed. Franklin died in 1790 at the age of 84.

Benjamin Franklin

George Clymer

Philadelphia patriot George Clymer was born in 1739; a year later he was orphaned. George was raised by wealthy relatives, William and Hannah Coleman. William Coleman was a friend of Benjamin Franklin. After graduating from the College of Philadelphia, Clymer's first job was in Coleman's counting house. He later became a partner in a mercantile business that was owned by Reese Meredith, his father-in-law.

Clymer became involved in local politics and actively supported the colonists' protests against British policies. He served as a member of the Pennsylvania Council of Safety and was elected to the Continental Congress. Clymer was a signer of the Declaration of Independence. During the war Clymer's home in Chester County was destroyed by the British. He moved his family to Princeton, New Jersey, and returned to Philadelphia alone. He aided Robert Morris in raising funds for the Revolution. He was also one of three commissioners sent by Congress to Fort Pitt to investigate attacks by hostile Indians; actually, the attacks had been instigated by the British.

At the Constitutional Convention, Clymer was a supporter of the policies favoring a strong central government. He was active on many committees and was held in high esteem by his peers.

Thomas Mifflin

The son of a wealthy Quaker merchant, Thomas Mifflin was born in Philadelphia in 1744. His early education took place at a local Quaker school. He later attended the College of Philadelphia. He graduated in 1760 and then traveled and studied abroad. Mifflin became a partner in a family mercantile business with his brother George.

Thomas Mifflin was an early champion of colonists' rights. He was a member of the Pennsylvania Assembly and was one of the youngest members of the First Continental Congress. He became major-general in the army and later became responsible for securing supplies for the troops stationed at Valley Forge. After the war, Mifflin returned to political affairs, serving in the Pennsylvania Assembly, as governor of Pennsylvania and as a delegate to the Constitutional Convention. Although he did not enter many debates, he was described as being a well-informed and intelligent speaker.

George Clymer

Thomas Mifflin

Gouverneur Morris

Gouverneur Morris was born in 1752 at his family's New York estate. After graduating from college, he practiced law. As a young man, Gouverneur lost his leg as a result of a hunting accident; the loss never handicapped him. He helped write the New York State Constitution in 1776. Two years later he served in the Continental Congress in Philadelphia and was active on many of its committees. When he was not re-elected to represent New York, he moved to Philadelphia. Shortly after that, he was appointed Superintendent of Finance for Congress (now the U.S. Treasury) by Robert Morris (no relation). It was Gouverneur Morris who planned the decimal system of coinage.

As a Pennsylvania delegate to the Constitutional Convention, Morris's skill with words impressed the other delegates so much that they requested that he be the one to put their ideas into words. In addition, he did the actual writing of the document.

Early in the convention he favored a strong central government controlled by the wealthy; he later changed his mind and concluded that the people should elect the executive branch of the government. Also, he thought the Senate should have more power than the Congress.

Robert Morris

Gouverneur Morris

Robert Morris

Robert Morris was born in England in 1734. His family first settled in Maryland when he was thirteen. He later moved to Philadelphia and got a job working for shipping merchants; he became a partner in the firm and by age twenty, he was very wealthy.

In 1765 Morris opposed the British Stamp Act. He was a signer of the Declaration of Independence and personally helped finance and raise money for food, clothing, and armaments for the Revolutionary Army. He served as Superintendent of Finance for the new country under the Articles of Confederation.

Morris represented Pennsylvania at the Constitutional Convention. Later he served as a senator from Pennsylvania. Once the best known and wealthiest of businessmen, he was jailed from 1798 to 1801 for bankruptcy. This weakened his spirit, and he died in poverty five years later.

James Wilson

James Wilson was born in Scotland in 1742 and moved to Carlisle, Pennsylvania, at the age of twenty-three.

Before becoming one of Pennsylvania's delegates to the Constitutional Convention, he had been a delegate to the First Continental Congress. He wrote a paper declaring that the British had no authority over the colonists and in 1776 he voted for independence. During several terms in Congress he worked to fortify the federal government. He strongly criticized the Articles of Confederation for their weaknesses.

Wilson is regarded by many as second only to Madison as a constitutional expert. He is given credit for many phrases, including "the Federal Republic." He assisted Gouverneur Morris in the drafting of the document. He originated the idea of the electoral college. Wilson argued strongly in favor of the direct popular vote for legislators from each state. "No government could long exist without the confidence of the people."

Wilson later served on the United States Supreme Court as an associate justice. He died in 1798.

James Wilson

NEW JERSEY

New Jersey was the third state to ratify the Constitution.
(December 18, 1787)

David Brearly   **Jonathan Dayton**   **William C. Houston**

William Livingston   **William Paterson**

David Brearly

David Brearly was born in 1745 in Spring Grove, New Jersey. At age thirty, he was arrested for treason because of his anti-British activity, but he was rescued by a mob. In 1776 he helped to write the New Jersey State Constitution. In 1779 he was chosen to be Chief Justice of the New Jersey Supreme Court.

As a delegate to the Constitutional Convention, Brearly opposed the Virginia Plan for states' representation; he and William Paterson, also of New Jersey, led the opposition to this plan. Brearly also served as chairperson of the Committee for Unfinished Business.

In 1789 Brearly was chosen a presidential elector from New Jersey. That same year he was named to a United States district court. He died a year later.

David Brearly

Jonathan Dayton

The youngest delegate to the Constitutional Convention, Jonathan Dayton was born in Elizabeth on October 16, 1760. He graduated from the College of New Jersey (now called Princeton University) in 1776. He then entered the military as an ensign in the Third New Jersey Regiment, which was commanded by his father. After the war, he became a lawyer and a member of the New Jersey Assembly.

During the Constitutional Convention, twenty-six-year-old Dayton voiced his opposition to slavery. He was said to be well-spoken but short of temper. Dayton served in the United States Congress from 1791 to 1799 and was a United States senator from 1799 to 1805.

Jonathan Dayton, for whom Dayton, Ohio, was named, owned large areas of land in Ohio. Unfortunately, Dayton later became implicated in the Aaron Burr conspiracy and was charged with a misdemeanor by the courts.

William Churchill Houston

William Churchill Houston was born around the year 1746. Not wealthy, he tutored while attending the College of New Jersey (now called Princeton University) to earn money for his expenses. He later became a professor of mathematics and philosophy at Princeton. Houston served as captain in the Revolutionary War. He then served in the Continental Congress until he became ill in 1781.

Houston represented New Jersey at the Annapolis Convention. He did not sign the Constitution, but he did instruct that his name be included on the report recommending it to the state legislature. He died in 1788 of tuberculosis, leaving a widow and four children.

Jonathan Dayton

William Livingston

William Paterson

William Livingston

New Jersey delegate William Livingston was born in Albany, New York, in 1723. He was the seventh son of a wealthy, land-owning family. His older brother Philip had been a signer of the Declaration of Independence. Livingston received private tutoring as a child and spent a year living with the Mohawk Indians as a young teenager. He entered Yale University in 1739, earning first a B.A. and then an M.A. three years later. Livingston continued his education in New York, studying law in the office of James Alexander. Although he became a successful lawyer, in 1772 he retired with his family to an estate in Elizabeth, New Jersey. Livingston and his wife Susan had thirteen children.

Livingston became very involved in New Jersey politics. He was elected to the First Continental Congress in 1774. At that time Livingston was described as a plain man, who wore his own hair instead of a wig. Livingston was re-elected to the Second Continental Congress and also commanded the New Jersey militia. He was elected governor of New Jersey.

While serving at the Constitutional Convention, Livingston was placed on committees to consider several important questions. One dealt with the slave trade, another with navigation acts, and another with taxation. Because Livingston was opposed to slavery, he introduced a resolution asking for a time limit to be established for the importation of slaves. Livingston did not often engage in debates on the floor of the convention, but he was a very important delegate.

William Paterson

Born in Ireland in 1745, young William Paterson came with his family to the colonies and settled in New Jersey. His father, Richard, was a tinware salesman. Paterson attended the College of New Jersey (now called Princeton University), receiving both a B.A. and an M.A. He studied law with Richard Stockton, a signer of the Declaration of Independence.

Paterson set up a law practice near Princeton and he represented Somerset County in the New Jersey Congress. In 1776 Paterson became an officer with the Minute Men of New Jersey and later became state attorney general. He resumed his law practice in New Brunswick and also served as a federal judge.

As a delegate to the Constitutional Convention, Paterson strongly opposed the establishment of a powerful national government. He said that New Jersey would never go along with the plan to give large states more votes than small states. He also opposed any encouragement of the slave trade. During the meeting Paterson proposed that the President be appointed by electors that would be chosen by the states.

After the Constitutional Convention, Paterson continued to serve the country as United States senator, as governor of New Jersey and as associate justice of the Supreme Court. Paterson, New Jersey, is named after him.

GEORGIA

Georgia was the fourth state to ratify the Constitution.
(January 2, 1788)

Abraham Baldwin   **William Few**

William Houstoun   **William Pierce**

Abraham Baldwin

The son of a blacksmith, Abraham Baldwin was born in Connecticut in 1754. He received his early education at a local school and continued his studies at Yale University, where he taught after graduation. During the Revolutionary War he served as a brigade chaplain. In 1783 Baldwin decided to study law and in 1784 he moved to Georgia to begin his law practice. As a member of the Georgia Assembly, Baldwin actively pursued the establishment of a state university. He was then elected to the Continental Congress, where he became involved in land and commerce decisions.

Baldwin served on a variety of committees during the Constitutional Convention: the Slave Trade Committee, the Navigation Acts Committee, and the Tax Committee; however, his most important vote had to do with the question of representation in Congress. Since roll call was taken in geographical order, Georgia was the last state called. The vote was tied between the large and small states. Although Georgia was a small state, Baldwin voted with the larger states for equal representation. Baldwin helped edit an early draft of the Constitution. He supported the concept of one President, given considerable power but responsible to the citizens.

In later years, Baldwin became a member of the United States House of Representatives and was appointed President of the University of Georgia. Although he never married, he was responsible for the education of six siblings and helped others to achieve an education or to start a business. Baldwin later served as a United States senator. When asked to comment on his achievements, he said that he considered his role as delegate to the Constitutional Convention the greatest service that he gave his country.

Abraham Baldwin

William Houstoun

William Few

William Few

Born in Maryland in 1748, William Few moved to North Carolina at an early age. The family settled in a rural area and Few learned about agriculture on the family farm. When a teacher established a small school in the area, Few attended for about one year; afterwards, Few continued to read on his own and acquired a great deal of knowledge on a variety of subjects. The Few family joined the Regulators, a group of farmers who were unhappy with unfair colonial taxation. Few moved to Georgia, where he became a justice of the peace in 1776. During the Revolutionary War, Few became a lieutenant colonel in the Georgia militia. He was a member of the Continental Congress from 1780 to 1783 and approved the decision of the Annapolis Convention to organize a Constitutional Convention in Philadelphia.

As a delegate to the Constitutional Convention, Few became a member of the Trade Exchange Committee. Although he was not an active debater during the meetings, he was described as dignified and well-spoken. He became a United States senator and later a member of the House of Representatives. When he left political life, he moved to New York, where he became active in the field of banking.

William Houstoun

William Houstoun was born in Georgia in 1757, the youngest of six children. He studied law in London and then returned to Georgia in 1782. He served in the Continental Congress from 1784 to 1786. As a delegate to the Constitutional Convention he favored more than one term for presidency. He opposed guaranteeing the states the right to their own constitutions. On the question of how the population would be counted, he was in favor of counting all inhabitants as part of the population. When he split with Baldwin on this vote, he brought the convention to a halt.

William Pierce

Georgia delegate William Pierce was born in Virginia in 1740. During the Revolutionary War, Pierce commanded an artillery company. He also served as an aide-de-camp to General Nathaniel Greene. After the war, Pierce established a trading company and exported rice and indigo.

Pierce entered politics in 1786 when he was elected to the Continental Congress. His greatest contributions to the Constitutional Convention were his meticulous notes that provided insightful impressions of the delegates. Pierce described Georgia delegate William Houstoun: "His person is striking, but as to his legal or political knowledge, he has very little to boast of." He characterized James Madison as a "gentleman of great modesty and a sweet temper."

Pierce supported the idea of a popular vote to elect senators and a vote by the state legislatures to elect members of the House of Representatives. Although Pierce represented Georgia, he personally supported issues that satisfied the needs of the majority of American citizens. He left the Convention before its completion in order to return to his duties in the Congress of New York.

CONNECTICUT

Connecticut was the fifth state to ratify the Constitution.
(January 9, 1788)

Oliver Ellsworth　　　**Roger Sherman**　　　**William Johnson**

Oliver Ellsworth

Oliver Ellsworth was born on April 29, 1745, in Windsor, Connecticut. He studied at Yale University but transferred to the College of New Jersey (now called Princeton University) from which he graduated in 1776. In addition to practicing law, he farmed and chopped wood to support himself and his wife. He was active in state politics and held several voluntary positions.

At the Constitutional Convention Ellsworth worked very hard with Roger Sherman and William Johnson to bring about a compromise between the small and large states in the argument regarding representation at the national level. The Connecticut Compromise, also called the Great Compromise, was accepted as the solution. Ellsworth played many roles and participated in many discussions. He served on the judiciary committee. The Judiciary Act of 1789 is credited mostly to him.

Ellsworth approved the draft of the Constitution, but he was called home to attend to personal business and was not present to sign the document in September. At the state convention Ellsworth opened the meeting with a long speech asking for approval of the Constitution.

Oliver Ellsworth and William Johnson served as Connecticut's first United States senators. Ellsworth later became the second Chief Justice of the United States Supreme Court.

Oliver Ellsworth

Roger Sherman

William Johnson

William Johnson

William Johnson was born in Stratford, Connecticut, in 1727. His father was a minister, and Johnson received his early education from him. Johnson entered Yale University at the age of thirteen and graduated with honors; he ranked third in a class of fourteen. Although his father wanted him to study the ministry, Johnson decided on a career in law. He continued his education at Yale and also at Harvard. In addition, he read law materials on his own. William Johnson was well respected for his knowledge about the law and soon became a very popular attorney. His law practice included clients from New York as well as from Connecticut. He studied further at King's College in New York and at Oxford University in London.

In 1760 Johnson entered politics as a selectman in Stratford. Later he served as a state assemblyman and was active in the protests against the Stamp Act. He was selected to be the Connecticut representative in London, where he gave the colony's point of view on the Townshend Acts. In 1748 he served on the Continental Congress, where he was a member of the Land Grant Committee.

At the outset of the Constitutional Convention, Johnson described the delegates as ''many of the most able men in America.'' Along with the other Connecticut members, Johnson worked for a compromise between the large and small states over representation. He opposed the slave trade along with Sherman and Ellsworth. Johnson and Ellsworth became Connecticut's first United States senators. Johnson later served as president of Columbia College. He was described as the ''Father of the Connecticut Bar.''

Roger Sherman

Roger Sherman was born in Massachusetts in 1721. He was first a cobbler, but later he became a lawyer, judge, and prosperous businessman. At age twenty-one he moved to Connecticut, where he bought land and became active in local politics. Although he was a conservative man, this Connecticut delegate was the only man to sign the four documents that formed the Republic: the Declaration of Rights and Grievances of the Colonies, the Declaration of Independence, the Articles of Confederation, and the Constitution.

Upon his arrival in Philadelphia for the Constitutional Convention, he thought that the Articles of Confederation could still be used with some revision; however, he quickly realized the need for a new governing document. It was Sherman who proposed the Connecticut Compromise, or Great Compromise, which was decided upon after much discussion and debate as the answer to several issues, especially that of representation.

Sherman later served in Congress from 1789 to 1791 and in the Senate from 1791 to 1793, when he died.

MASSACHUSETTS

Massachusetts was the sixth state to ratify the Constitution.
(February 6, 1788)

Elbridge Gerry   **Nathaniel Gorham**   **Rufus King**

Elbridge Gerry

Born in Marblehead, Massachusetts, in 1744, Elbridge Gerry was the son of a successful merchant. After he graduated from Harvard in 1762, he entered his father's business. Gerry switched to politics in 1772 and became a member of the state House of Representatives. He assisted Samuel Adams in several of the colonists' causes. He served on government committees, such as the Committee of Supply and the Committee of Safety. Gerry was the author of a state bill that aided the development of armed ships to defend the seacoasts.

Gerry was sent to the Continental Congress in 1776; he served on the Treasury Committee. He was an enthusiastic signer of the Declaration of Independence and the Articles of Confederation. He acquired a national reputation as a respected legislator.

However, Gerry's views at the Constitutional Convention often ran contrary to the general opinion of the membership. He opposed the idea of a popular election for the President. He felt that the President should be elected by the state governors. Gerry spoke of an excess of democracy in the proposed national government. He attacked the concept of a strong national government and he did not approve of federal control of the militia. Gerry advocated an annual election of representatives and a limitation upon the ability of the federal government to tax citizens. Because of his objections, Gerry refused to sign the Constitution and recommended a second convention.

Gerry later served as an ambassador to France and as governor of Massachusetts. The term *gerrymandering* was named after Elbridge Gerry. Gerrymandering is the division of a geographical area into voting districts in such a way that it benefits a particular party in an election. Gerry was elected Vice President under James Madison.

Nathaniel Gorham

Rufus King

Elbridge Gerry

Nathaniel Gorham

The eldest of five children, Nathaniel Gorham was born in 1738 in Charlestown, Massachusetts. By about 1760 he had become a successful merchant. Gorham served for more than five years in the Massachusetts Assembly and then the Massachusetts House of Representatives. He was instrumental in writing the state constitution and was a member of the Continental Congress.

As a delegate to the Constitutional Convention, Gorham served as chairman of the Committee of the Whole; he also served on the Committee of Detail. Gorham opposed the motion to restrict the Senate to the area of budgeting, raising, and appropriating money. He felt that both houses should conduct all kinds of business. He also opposed a restriction upon who could run for congressional office. Gorham made several proposals that became part of the Constitution, including the proposal that senators be elected to six-year terms. Gorham supported the appointment of federal judges by the executive branch and the ratification of the Constitution by convention or assembly in each state rather than by the legislatures.

Rufus King

Massachusetts delegate Rufus King was born on a farm in Maine in 1755. At that time the area was part of the Massachusetts Bay Colony. Rufus attended private elementary school and continued his education at Harvard, where he graduated first in his class. At Newburyport, he began the study of law with Theophilus Parsons. During the Revolutionary War King established a thriving law practice in Newburyport and became active in local politics. At the age of twenty-nine he became a representative to the Continental Congress. There he spoke out strongly against slavery. He also was active on several committees, including one that decided territorial claims.

As a delegate to the Constitutional Convention, King was at first opposed to a strong national government. His ideas changed under the influence of Alexander Hamilton. Rufus King served on a committee that decided the proportional representation in the House of Representatives and on the Navigation Acts Committee. He was a supporter of the Virginia Plan and of an extended term of office for the President. King was a vocal opponent of the slave trade. He also disliked the plan that provided the President with an advisory council. During the meetings, King carefully recorded the happenings. His well-documented records proved a great insight into the workings of the Convention.

In 1788 King moved to New York. He became a prominent Federalist and served as one of New York's first United States senators. He held that office from 1789 to 1796 and again from 1813 to 1825.

MARYLAND

Maryland was the seventh state to ratify the Constitution.
(April 16, 1788)

Daniel Carroll   **Daniel of St. Thomas Jenifer**   **James McHenry**

Daniel Carroll

Daniel Carroll was born in Upper Marlboro, Maryland, in 1730. He was given a Catholic education in Flanders at the Saint Omers School. Daniel's brother John was an archbishop of Baltimore.

After his years of study and travel in Europe, Carroll returned home to manage the family plantation and to take part in public life. He was elected to Congress in 1781 when the members were voting upon the Articles of Confederation. Maryland was the last state to ratify the new laws because of objections to western territorial claims by other states. During his term in Congress, Carroll favored strong central government policies.

At the Constitutional Convention, Carroll was a dedicated delegate. He was assigned to work on three committees. He supported the electoral method of choosing a President. He also supported the motion that with two-thirds of the members in agreement, a member of Congress could be expelled. He objected to the limited powers that Congress had been given under the Articles of Confederation and argued for a more powerful government under the Constitution. Carroll continued to serve in public life until his death in 1795.

Daniel of St. Thomas Jenifer

Named for his English grandfather, Dan Jenifer was born in Charles County, Maryland, in 1723. After receiving a good education, his first post was as justice of the peace for Charles County. Jenifer was chosen president of the Maryland Council of Safety, which advanced the colonists' causes against Britain. He was elected to the state senate of Maryland and was also sent to the Continental Congress.

At the Constitutional Convention, Jenifer was an active participant in the debates. He supported a three-year term for all representatives and favored prohibiting senators to hold other offices; he was opposed to merely amending the Articles. Jenifer, who never married, was described as a quiet man who was always in good humor.

Daniel Carroll

Daniel of St. Thomas Jenifer

James McHenry

James McHenry

Maryland delegate James McHenry was born in Ireland in 1753 and educated in Dublin. He arrived in Philadelphia in 1771 to begin life in America. He continued his education in Delaware and then studied medicine with Dr. Benjamin Rush in Philadelphia. He became an ardent patriot and served as a military doctor during the Revolutionary War. He was appointed aide to George Washington and to the Marquis de Lafayette. In 1781 McHenry was at first in favor of amending the Articles. During the convention debates he argued that Congress was to be given too much power in taxing and regulating trade. He made a motion asking that the President be given the power to convene Congress on very special occasions. Although McHenry had some objections to parts of the Constitution, he felt that overall it was "for the general good."

Henry became a state senator and later secretary of war under Washington. In 1814 Francis Scott Key wrote the "Star Spangled Banner" at Fort McHenry, which had been named after this delegate.

SOUTH CAROLINA

South Carolina was the eighth state to ratify the Constitution.
(May 23, 1788)

Pierce Butler   **Charles Cotesworth Pinckney**

Charles Pinckney III   **John Rutledge**

Pierce Butler

The third son of a noble family, Pierce Butler was born in Ireland in 1744. His father was a member of Parliament. After serving in the British army in Boston from 1761 to 1762, he married and moved to South Carolina. He retired from the army in 1763 and served in several positions in the South Carolina government from 1778 to 1787.

A few days after the Constitutional Convention began, Butler moved that the proceedings not be interrupted because of the absence of members and that there should be no unofficial news or progress reports issued by any individuals. The members were to keep notes, etc., safe and secret. These motions were adopted as part of the rules of procedure.

Butler was in favor of the Virginia Plan, which proposed that the states' representation be based upon the entire population, whether freeman or slave. He also argued in favor of Oliver Ellsworth's plan of direct taxation to support the national government.

Butler did a great deal of volunteer work for the convention and as a result became very ill; nevertheless, he confided to a friend that his work was well worth the time and effort if it helped to make the Constitutional Convention a success.

After the convention, Butler served as a United States senator from South Carolina. He died in Philadelphia in 1822.

Pierce Butler

Charles Cotesworth Pinckney

South Carolina delegate Charles Cotesworth Pinckney was born to a prominent Charleston family in 1746. His father had served as the colony's justice officer and later as a commissioner representing South Carolina in London. Charles was sent to England for his education. He studied at Westminster and later became a law student at the Middle Temple. When he returned to South Carolina in 1770, he set up a successful law practice and became active in public affairs.

Pinckney was an ardent patriot and placed himself on many Revolutionary committees. During the war he became a lieutenant colonel and later attained the rank of general. He took part in the Battles of Brandywine and Germantown, as well as many smaller battles throughout the South. After the war, Pinckney entered politics, serving as a member of the state assembly.

Pinckney was sent to the Constitutional Convention, where he earned the reputation of being a talented debater. When he first arrived, he made it clear that he believed it to be the delegates' duty to revise the Articles of Confederation completely. He commented, "Otherwise, they might as well pack up and go home." Pinckney opposed setting a time limit for halting the slave trade. He thought that his state would be reluctant to ratify the Constitution if such a clause were included. He was in favor of allowing a four-year term of office for senators.

Pinckney returned to an active private law practice before being appointed a minister to France. He also served as a major general in the United States Army. He was an unsuccessful candidate for both President and Vice-president.

John Rutledge

Charles Pinckney

Charles Cotesworth Pinckney

Charles Pinckney III

The son of a wealthy, land-owning family, Charles Pinckney was born in Charleston, South Carolina, in 1757. He was a cousin to Charles Cotesworth Pinckney, also a delegate to the Constitutional Convention. Charles's family had hoped to send him to London to study law, but the Revolutionary War prevented that from happening. Instead, he received his law education in South Carolina and was admitted to the bar there. As a Patriot and member of the South Carolina militia, Pinckney took part in the seige of Savannah and was taken prisoner during the Battle of Charleston.

After the Revolutionary War, Pinckney returned to the practice of law and was sent to the state legislature as well. As a member of the Continental Congress, he was involved with the system of collecting revenue; he urged stronger federal powers to help the nation solve its financial difficulties. He opposed the Articles because they failed to give the federal government enough power to administer to the needs of its citizens.

Pinckney was an outstanding orator and was recognized for his intelligence at the Constitutional Convention. He was a member of the committee that suggested procedural rules for the Convention. During the Convention he submitted his own plan for the establishment of three branches of government and Congress. Although similar to Randolph's plan, it also called for three divisions of senators, each with differing terms of office. At the age of twenty-nine, Pinckney was the second youngest delegate at the Convention. He spoke out against setting a limit on slave trade and wanted all slaves counted in a population census. Pinckney suggested many powers and propositions that were later included in the Constitution. They included freedom of the press, the ability to override an executive veto, rules for patents and copyrights, and the abolishment of religious tests for national employees. Pinckney later served as governor of South Carolina and as a United States senator.

John Rutledge

The oldest of seven children, John Rutledge was born in Charleston, South Carolina, in 1739. Privately tutored at first, he continued his education in law at the Middle Temple in London. Rutledge returned to Charleston to practice law. He was regarded as a brilliant attorney and soon became very successful. He acquired five large plantations in less than fifteen years.

During the Revolutionary War, he became governor of South Carolina and was an active Patriot. When the British seized his property and burned his home, Rutledge narrowly escaped capture. Rutledge was elected to the Continental Congress in 1782 and 1783 and served on many important committees at those meetings.

While at the Constitutional Convention, Rutledge voiced his opinions on several issues. He opposed judicial appointments by the President, but he approved of having representatives elected to a House of Representatives according to population. Rutledge felt that there should be a two-year term for representatives. An unusual proposal by Rutledge was that wealth or property ownership should be a qualification for a member of Congress. Rutledge spoke forcefully against the question of stopping or taxing the slave trade. He served in various judicial posts until his death.

NEW HAMPSHIRE

New Hampshire was the ninth state to ratify the Constitution.
(June 21, 1788)

Nicholas Gilman   John Langdon

Nicholas Gilman

Nicholas Gilman was born in Exeter to an well-established New Hampshire family on August 3, 1755. He took part in many battles of the Revolutionary War.

Although he served well at the Constitutional Convention in Philadelphia, there is nothing outstanding that is specifically credited to him. He participated in the new government he helped to form. Gilman served as a representative in Congress from 1789 to 1797 and later as a United States senator from New Hampshire from 1804 until his death in 1814.

John Langdon

John Langdon was born in 1741 on his family's farm near Portsmouth, New Hampshire. He was apprenticed in a "counting house" and later became a ship's captain and then a very successful merchant. Langdon was an early strong supporter of the movement against the British. He led the first attack against a British fort, served in the militia, and helped to finance and form the first naval forces. It was Langdon who sent John Paul Jones on his first missions. He personally financed a group that defeated the British at Saratoga, New York; this defeat was a turning point in the War for Independence. Langdon also served in the Continental Congress.

John Langdon so strongly believed in the Constitutional Convention that when the state of New Hampshire failed to come up with the money for the delegates to stay in Philadelphia, Langdon paid for his own expenses and those of delegate Nicholas Gilman.

After serving as a delegate at the Constitutional Convention, he was elected to the Senate and he was chosen president of that organization. It was Langdon who wrote to George Washington informing him of his election as President of the United States. He continued to serve his state and his country in many ways, both public and private. He corresponded regularly with five presidents, who also visited him at his home in Portsmouth. This home is open to the public. Langdon died on September 18, 1819, and was given full military honors.

Nicholas Gilman

John Langdon

VIRGINIA

Virginia was the tenth state to ratify the Constitution.
(June 25, 1788)

John Blair   **James Madison**   **George Mason**

Edmund Randolph   **George Washington**

John Blair

John Blair was born in Williamsburg in 1732. He became one of the most respected men in Virginia. After receiving his law degree, he served in the Virginia House of Burgesses from 1765 to 1769. He served on the committee to write the Virginia Bill of Rights and the state constitution.

At the Constitutional Convention Blair did not participate in the discussions or the debates except to vote. He opposed the proposal of a single office for the executive branch. Later he served as a justice on the United States Supreme Court. He died in Williamsburg in 1800.

James Madison

The son of a wealthy landowner, James Madison was born in Virginia in 1751. He attended the College of New Jersey, today called Princeton University. He was a brilliant student; it took him only two years to complete a course that took most others four years! Madison was elected to the Second Continental Congress; at twenty-nine he was the youngest member. He was determined to help the thirteen colonies become a free nation and to grow in strength, economics, territory, and freedom.

As a delegate to the Constitutional Convention, Madison worked for reform in a calm, systematic manner. It was Madison's urging that convinced Washington to become a part of the Virginia delegation to the Constitutional Convention. Many of the delegates offered valuable suggestions during the discussions and debates. It is generally agreed that more than anyone else, Madison was chiefly responsible for producing the Constitution from their labors. This earned him the title "Father of the Constitution." He was able to persuade many delegates because of his knowledge of constitutional law and his clear reasoning. He reminded the other delegates that their solutions should be based on the national interests of a permanent nature, rather than upon the temporary interests of a few states.

In addition to his other duties, Madison was a careful recorder of the convention proceedings. By sitting front and center, directly in front of the convention president, Madison was able to hear and see all the "goings on." He was present every day and missed very little of the sessions. His notes were much more complete than the official records.

Following the convention, Madison worked for the ratification of the Constitution in Virginia. He later was elected as fourth President of the United States. Most historians feel his best contribution was as "Father of the Constitution."

George Mason

George Mason was born in 1725 in Fairfax County, Virginia. He was privately tutored. During the 1750's and 1760's he ran his large farm and served in local political offices. He was partly responsible for sending Lewis and Clark on their famous expedition to explore the Northwest Territory.

As a delegate to the Constitutional Convention, Mason agreed (most of the time) that there was a need for a new document. There are several issues on which we have his voting record. He was in favor of giving all citizens, regardless of their wealth, the right to vote for their national leaders. He fought vigorously against giving the power of veto to the executive branch. He violently opposed slavery. When the work of the Constitution was complete, he refused to sign because it did not have a Bill of Rights and because it did not prohibit slavery. When he returned to Virginia, he worked against ratification. Mason did live to see the Bill of Rights added. He died in 1792.

George Mason

James Madison

John Blair

Edmund Randolph

Edmund Randolph was born near Williamsburg in 1753 to a prominent and politically active family. His father, uncle, and grandfather had all served as the king's attorneys in the colonies. His uncle, Peyton Randolph, had been president of the First Continental Congress. Edmund graduated from William and Mary College in Williamsburg and studied law with his father. For a short time he served as a military aide to General Washington. He established a successful law practice and was elected mayor of Williamsburg. He also served as attorney general of the state. Randolph helped to draft Virginia's constitution and he became governor of Virginia at the age of thirty-nine.

At the Constitutional Convention, Randolph presented the Virginia Plan, which provided a plan of government that won favor with the larger states. It provided among other things that the population of each state would determine how many representatives it could send to congress. Randolph opposed the election of a single President. His preference was for a committee of three men to lead the nation. He also felt that Congress did not have to agree to Constitutional amendments. Randolph actively opposed the limitation on the slave trade. He said that he hoped the convention could find some "middle ground." Randolph served on an important committee that offered a compromise and broke the deadlock between those who favored his Virginia Plan and those who favored the New Jersey Plan.

Randolph apologized but felt that he could not sign the Constitution because of "its defects." When Virginia adopted the Constitution, however, Randolph gave it his support. He later became attorney general under Washington and in 1794 he became secretary of state. He also served as legal counsel for Aaron Burr during Burr's treason trial.

Edmund Randolph

George Washington

George Washington was born on February 22, 1732, on the family farm in Westmoreland County, Virginia. He had, at most, seven or eight years of formal education. He became a surveyor's apprentice at age fifteen and was named Culpepper County surveyor for five years. At age twenty he sought and received a commission in the Virginia militia. He distinguished himself in the French and Indian War.

From 1759 to 1773 Washington devoted himself to improving his farms, serving as a judge of the County Court and becoming a popular and learned legislator in the Virginia House of Burgesses. It was in 1759 that he married Martha Custis. They would live on Washington's plantation in Mount Vernon.

During the Revolutionary War, Washington served as the commander-in-chief of the Continental Army. He refused to accept pay. After the war he returned to Mount Vernon and resumed his private life.

He was convinced by James Madison to be part of the Constitutional Convention as a Virginia delegate. He was unanimously elected president of the Convention on May 25, 1787. It was his duty to oversee debates, keep speakers to the point, and insure that everyone follow the rules of order as agreed upon by the delegates. One of the rules to which the delegates agreed was that of secrecy. At one time Washington spoke sternly to the delegates about a ''leak'' in their ''wall of secrecy.'' On a daily basis, he spoke very little, but his presence helped hold things together. After the work of the Convention was completed, he worked hard in Virginia for ratification of the Constitution.

In 1788 Washington was elected first President of the United States under the new Constitution. He was re-elected in 1792. He was commissioned Commander-in-Chief of the United States Armies in 1796 when President Adams asked him to organize a national army.

On December 12, 1799, Washington wrote to Alexander Hamilton about the need for a national military academy. Two days later he died at his home as a result of what modern doctors believe was a strep infection of his throat. He was sixty-seven years of age and had lived an exciting life during most exciting times.

George Washington

NEW YORK

New York was the eleventh state to ratify the Constitution.
(June 26, 1788)

Alexander Hamilton   **John Lansing**   **Robert Yates**

Alexander Hamilton

Alexander Hamilton was born in Jamaica, West Indies, in 1757. He came to New York at the age of fifteen. During the Revolutionary War he joined as an aide-de-camp for General Washington. He later attained military status with the rank of colonel and led the charge at Yorktown.

As early as 1780 Hamilton campaigned for the need for a Constitutional Convention. He wrote editorials and newspaper articles; he gave speeches and addressed the New York state legislature. He worked closely with James Madison at the Annapolis Convention in Maryland to strengthen the national government, especially in areas of business and trade. The report that was issued from Annapolis was the forerunner of the Constitutional Convention.

It was Hamilton who thought that the first order of business should be to decide if the United States would be just a loosely associated group of states or if the individual states would join together as one nation governed by one government. After a debate, a resolution was passed to form one national government rather than to revise the Articles of Confederation. As a delegate to the Constitutional Convention Alexander Hamilton proposed broad national powers, including a lifetime term for the executive (President)! When the document was completed, Alexander Hamilton and Gouverneur Morris seconded Benjamin Franklin's motion to recognize it and sign it.

Hamilton's battle for the Constitution was far from won. He returned to New York where he faced opposition from a powerful governor. Hamilton led the fight to have the Constitution ratified. He sought the help of John Jay and James Madison. The three wrote letters to the public in defense of the Constitution. The letters were published in different newspapers two to four times a week. Hamilton is given credit for more than two-thirds of the eighty-five letters. Known as *The Federalist Papers,* the letters offered valuable examples of how the Constitution would work. The assembly ratified the Constitution by a slim margin.

Alexander Hamilton

In 1789 President Washington appointed Hamilton as the first secretary of the treasury. In 1804 Hamilton was challenged to a duel by Aaron Burr and killed.

John Lansing

John Lansing was born in Albany in 1754. In 1775 he began practicing law. He served in the New York militia and later in the New York assembly. He also served in the Continental Congress and as mayor of Albany.

At the Constitutional Convention he supported William Paterson of New Jersey, who was the spokesperson for the small states in their opposition to the Virginia Plan. He claimed that he represented New York in saying that New York did not want to form a federal government at the expense of the state's independence. He voted against having two branches of Congress. He wanted the Bill of Rights to be included as a condition for ratification. On July 10, 1787, John Lansing and fellow New York delegate Robert Yates left Philadelphia in opposition to the creation of the system of government that had been proposed. Lansing became one of the most active Anti-Federalists.

Lansing later served as judge of the New York Supreme Court. In December 1829, while in New York City, he mysteriously disappeared from his hotel and was never seen nor heard from again.

Robert Yates

Robert Yates was born January 27, 1738, in Schenectady, New York. He began his law practice in Albany in 1760. An early Patriot, he held several positions before and during the War for Independence. He was on the committee that wrote the New York state constitution.

Yates attended the Constitutional Convention from May 30 to July 10, 1787. He and John Lansing left Philadelphia. In a letter to Governor Clinton of New York, they explained that they opposed any system of government which wanted to establish supreme legislative, executive, and judicial branches. Yates and Lansing were accused by George Washington as being narrow-minded and only interested in preserving states' rights. He said they were not interested in forming a nation.

Yates died in 1801. In 1821 his wife published his notes, which are second only to those of James Madison in importance.

NORTH CAROLINA

North Carolina was the twelfth state to ratify the Constitution.
(November 21, 1789)

William Blount   **Richard Dobbs Spaight**   **Hugh Williamson**

William Blount

The eldest of eight children, William Blount was born in North Carolina in 1749. His father, Jacob Blount, was a plantation owner and also a trader. During the Revolutionary War, William fought with the North Carolina Regiment and became the paymaster for the local militia. Actively involved in state politics, he was elected to the state assembly in 1781 and again in 1783. Along with his brothers, he developed a successful mercantile business and became interested in land development. He bought large tracts of western acreage. Blount served in the Continental Congress and was a member for several years.

At the Constitutional Convention, Blount favored states' rights and added to discussions concerning western expansion from his own experiences. He was described as being a man of reason and always willing to compromise.

Blount later became governor of the new territory that would later become the state of Tennessee. He helped the area prepare for statehood and was elected as one of the first United States senators from that state.

Richard Dobbs Spaight

Richard Dobbs Spaight was born in New Bern, North Carolina, in 1758. His father had been involved in colonial politics, and his mother was the sister of Arthur Dobbs, a governor of North Carolina. Spaight was sent to Ireland and then to Scotland for his education; he graduated from the University of Glasgow. When he returned to America, Spaight joined the Revolutionary forces in South Carolina. He became a member of the state House of Representatives during the period from 1785 to 1787. Spaight was a member of the Continental Congress and the Committee of States.

Spaight was an energetic member of the Constitutional Convention. He asked that members be allowed to reconsider issues and change their votes if necessary. Spaight argued for election of the Senate members by state legislatures and thought that seven years was an appropriate term of office for a senator. He wanted Congress to appoint a President and he believed that the term should be six or seven years. Spaight was opposed to an equality of votes in the Senate.

Spaight was governor of North Carolina from 1792 to 1795. He died in 1802 as a result of a duel with John Stanley.

Hugh Williamson

Hugh Williamson was born in Pennsylvania in 1735. He was a man of varied professions. He studied theology at the College of Philadelphia and after graduating became a preacher. He soon desired a change in occupation and studied medicine and mathematics. Williamson received an M.D. at the University of Ultricht in 1776. He also became a member of Benjamin Franklin's Philosophical Society in Philadelphia, where he studied comets among other things.

Williamson was in Europe when the Revolutionary War erupted. On the way home his ship was captured by British seamen; however, he escaped capture. He then traveled to North Carolina, where he joined his brother in a mercantile business. During the war he resumed his medical practice, administering care to the North Carolina Militia. Williamson was a member of the Continental Congress, where he served on many committees and was an ardent supporter of a peacetime army.

As a delegate to the Constitutional Convention, Williamson was an active speaker. He voted in favor of the slavery compromise, for he was personally against slavery. During the meetings, he suggested that a two-thirds vote of each house be required in order to override a presidential veto. He also insisted that the Constitution allow for a jury in civil trials. Although he initially opposed the Great Compromise, he later voted for it.

Williamson moved to New York and made contributions in the fields of politics, writing, medicine, and science until his death in 1819.

Hugh Williamson

Richard Spaight

William Blount

SECTION III:
Vocabulary Activities

These activities are designed to reinforce the many terms which must be understood in order to have a basic understanding of the United States Constitution and its formation.

Constitutional Vocabulary List

It is necessary to be familiar with the following terms in order to complete the activities in this section. Write the definition of each word in the space provided. Use your dictionary or your social studies textbook if necessary.

amend

amendment

article

Articles of Confederation

Bill of Rights

capitol

checks and balances

compromise

confederation

Congress

constitution

continental

delegate

economic

executive

federal

Federalist

framework

Great Compromise

House of Representatives

Independence Hall

interpret

judicial

legislative

militia

New Jersey Plan

Northwest Ordinance

preamble

representative

republic

Senate

Shay's Rebellion

tranquility

unconstitutional

Virginia Plan

veto

Constitutional Word Shapes

Which of the words from your Constitution Vocabulary List would form the following shapes?

Example: *constitution* looks like this:

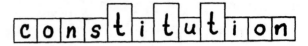

1.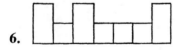

2.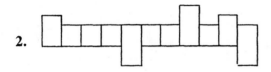

3.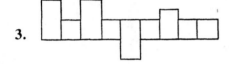

4.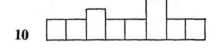

5.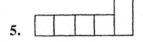

6.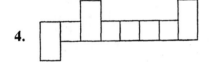

7.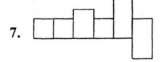

8.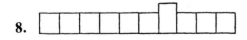

9.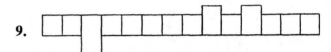

10.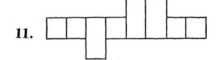

11.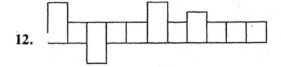

12.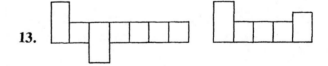

13.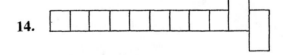

14.

15.

Word Scramble

Can you identify the vocabulary words shown scrambled in the Liberty Bell?

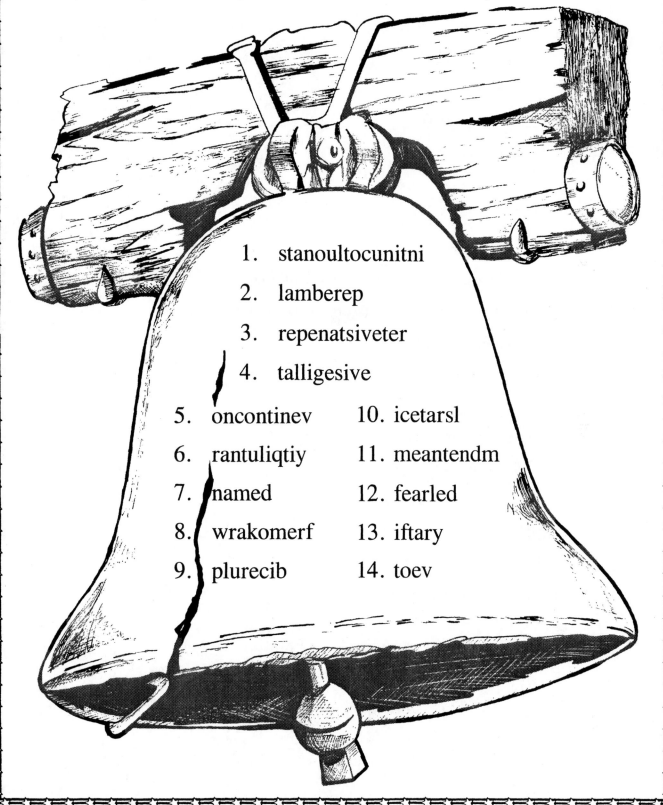

1. stanoultocunitni
2. lamberep
3. repenatsiveter
4. talligesive
5. oncontinev
6. rantuliqtiy
7. named
8. wrakomerf
9. plurecib
10. icetarsl
11. meantendm
12. fearled
13. iftary
14. toev

Constitutional Match-ups

Match the vocabulary words to the appropriate definitions.

1. _____ delegate

2. _____ militia

3. _____ judicial

4. _____ unconstitutional

5. _____ preamble

6. _____ ratify

7. _____ Federalist

8. _____ Northwest Ordinance

9. _____ Connecticut

10. _____ amend

11. _____ tranquility

12. _____ veto

A. To change in an attempt to improve

B. A person authorized to act as a representative of another

C. A member of a political party that favors a strong central government

D. Citizens with military training

E. An introductory statement

F. To approve

G. Of or about the law and the courts

H. Free from disturbance or turmoil

I. The power to prohibit, especially the President's power to disallow a proposed law

J. Name of plan for dividing territories into new states

K. Name of plan that settled the issue of representation in the national Congress

L. Not in accordance with the Constitution

True or False?

If you have mastered the vocabulary list, you will be able to determine whether the following statements are true or false. Read each statement, paying careful attention to the word in **bold** in each. Circle T (true) or F (false) for each statement.

T F 1. Our federal **legislative** body usually meets at the court house.

T F 2. The **preamble** to the Constitution is also known as the twenty-second amendment.

T F 3. The President has the power to **veto** legislation.

T F 4. The **Constitutional Convention** met in Philadelphia in 1787.

T F 5. James Madison was a **Federalist.**

T F 6. The Constitutional Convention met in **Independence Hall.**

T F 7. The **Supreme Court** is the highest court in the United States.

T F 8. When you **ratify** an amendment, you cancel it.

T F 9. The **Connecticut Compromise** gave one half of Rhode Island to Massachusetts.

T F 10. A **militia** was a group of people opposed to the Constitution.

T F 11. The **executive** branch of the federal government is the most powerful.

T F 12. A treaty with England was approved by the **Articles of Confederation.**

T F 13. The form of government in the United States is known as a **republic.**

T F 14. The office of vice-president is a **federal** position.

T F 15. The President of the United States may decide if a law is **unconstitutional.**

Constitutional Crossword

Use the words from your Constitutional Vocabulary List to create a crossword puzzle. Try to use as many words as you can. Use the grid below to figure out your puzzle. (You might want to use pencil until you are sure the puzzle is the way you want it.) Number the spaces horizontally and vertically. Darken the boxes you are not using. When you are sure the puzzle is the way you want it, copy the numbers and the darkened spaces onto the grid on the next page. Write your clues in the space provided. Exchange with a classmate to solve.

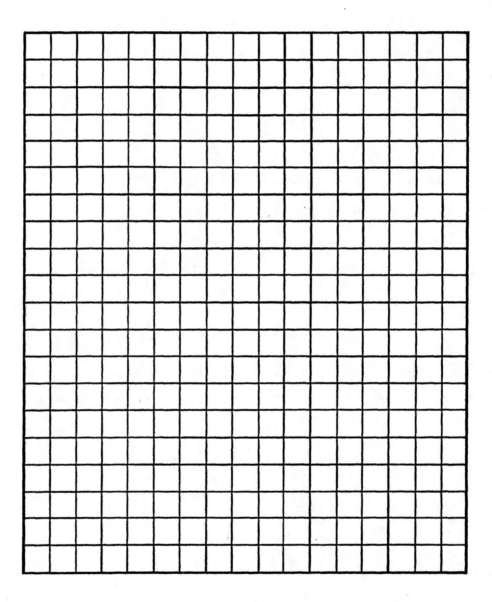

Constitutional Crossword

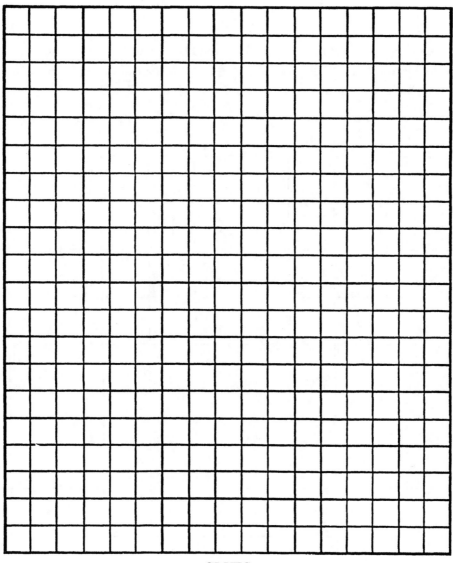

CLUES

Across:

Down:

Constitutional Word Find

Use the words from your Constitutional Vocabulary List to create a word-find puzzle. You may place the words in a straight line in any direction. Be sure to list the words in the space provided. Exchange with a classmate to solve.

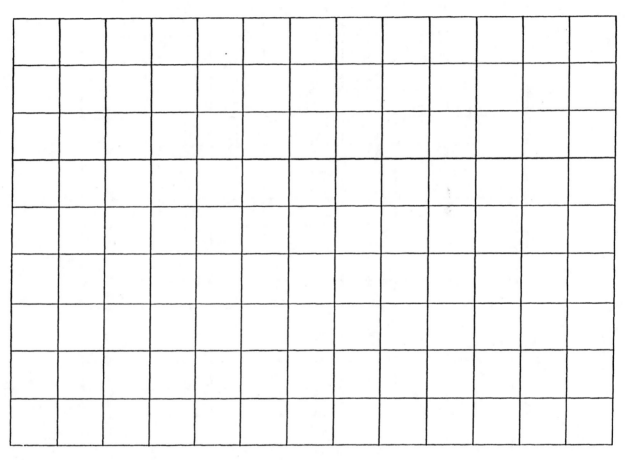

Find the following words:

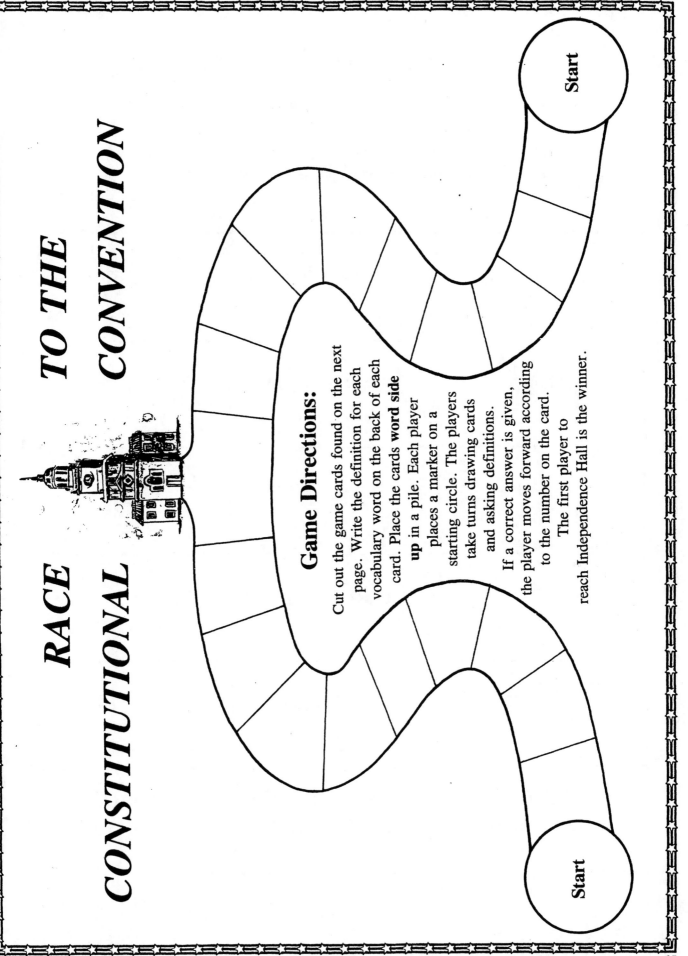

RACE
CONSTITUTIONAL

TO THE
CONVENTION

Start

Start

Game Directions:

Cut out the game cards found on the next page. Write the definition for each vocabulary word on the back of each card. Place the cards **word side up** in a pile. Each player places a marker on a starting circle. The players take turns drawing cards and asking definitions. If a correct answer is given, the player moves forward according to the number on the card. The first player to reach Independence Hall is the winner.

Race to the Constitutional Convention

Game Cards

Cut the cards apart. Write the appropriate definition on the back of each card. Place the vocabulary cards with the word side up in a pile near the game board.

PREAMBLE 2	VETO 2	RATIFY 2
FEDERAL 1	TRANQUILITY 3	JUDICIAL 1
AMEND 1	LEGISLATIVE 1	CONFEDERA- TION 2
DELEGATES 1	COMPROMISE 1	FRAMEWORK 1
REPRESEN- TATIVE 1	EXECUTIVE 1	CONVENTION 1
SHAY'S REBELLION 3	CONNECTICUT COMPROMISE 3	BILL OF RIGHTS 2

SECTION IV:
Critical- and Creative-
Thinking
Activities

These activities are designed to help develop students' higher-level thinking skills as well as to increase students' understanding of the United States Constitution.

Constitutional Riddles

Many people played important roles in the development of the United States Constitution. Select one of them and create clues to his or her identity. Be sure to make your first clue general and the following clues more specific. Try your luck with the example below.

1. Grew up on a farm
2. Married a widow with two children
3. Worked as a surveyor
4. Fought in the French and Indian Wars
5. Was Commander of Colonial Army

How many clues did you need to solve the riddle?

Now create a riddle of your own in the space below.
Clues:

1. _____

2. _____

4. _____

5. _____

   I am _____

In the second part of this activity you must personify one of the amendments, giving clues regarding its origins, its development, and its applications to everyday life in the United States. Your classmates will then try to determine the specific amendment using the information given in your clues. Use the form below to organize your clues.

My early supporters include: _____

_____

I guarantee that: _____

_____

Some ways I work in our everyday lives may include: _____

_____

_____

   I am amendment number _____

Making Conversation

Create an imaginary dialogue that might have taken place between two characters from the Constitutional period. You may choose two noted leaders or two ordinary citizens. Research an important issue to help you obtain facts for your conversation. Will your dialogue be friendly, or will it contain a lively debate?

_____

_____

_____

_____

_____

_____

_____

_____

_____

_____

_____

Constitutional Categories Game

In this activity you are to fill in the grid with words that begin with the letters on the left. These words must fit into the categories listed above the grid. You may put more than one word in each box. Compare your completed grid with those of your classmates. Score two points for words that no one else recorded; all other answers earn one point each.

	Vocabulary	People	Places/Events
A			
M			
E			
N			
D			

*Score*_____   *Name*_____

Constitutional Fact or Opinion

Test your ability to distinguish fact from opinion. Remember, a fact is a statement that is based upon positive knowledge; it can be objectively proved. An opinion is a belief or conclusion held without positive knowledge or proof.

Write F (fact) or O (opinion) for each statement.

_____ 1. The first ten amendments are called the Bill of Rights.

_____ 2. The judicial branch of the government has the most power.

_____ 3. George Washington was a brilliant leader.

_____ 4. The United States federal government has three branches.

_____ 5. Benjamin Franklin was the oldest delegate.

_____ 6. Representatives from twelve states attended the Constitutional Convention.

_____ 7. The federal government is too powerful.

_____ 8. James Madison is called the Father of the Constitution.

_____ 9. James Madison deserves the nickname Father of the Constitution.

_____ 10. Delaware was the first state to ratify the Constitution.

_____ 11. The Constitution was signed on September 17, 1787.

_____ 12. The Bill of Rights is the most important part of the Constitution.

_____ 13. The opening statement of the Constitution is called the Preamble.

_____ 14. The twenty-second amendment limits the number of terms for President.

Write a Letter

You are an assistant, clerk, or delegate away from home to attend the Constitutional Convention during the summer of 1787. Write a letter to a friend or family member back home. In your letter describe the conditions, foods, habits, events, and people you have encountered at the convention.

July 27, 1787

Dear _____,

Interpreting the Constitution

For this activity you are given some excerpts from the Constitution. What do you think the framers of the Constitution meant by these statements? Read the *italic phrases* and rewrite them in your own words. Use your dictionary to help you!

I. We the people of the United States, *in order to form a more perfect Union,* establish justice, *insure domestic tranquility,* provide for the common defense, promote the general welfare, and *secure the blessings of Liberty to ourselves and our posterity,* do ordain and establish this Constitution for the United States of America.

1. _____

2. _____

3. _____

II. Congress shall make no law respecting an establishment of religion, or prohibiting the free exercise thereof; or *abridging the freedom of speech,* or of the press; or the *right of the people peaceably to assemble,* and to petition the Government for a redress of grievances.

1. _____

2. _____

III. The *executive power shall be vested in a President of the United States of America.* He shall hold his office during the term of four years, together with the Vice-President, chosen for the same term.

1. _____

IV. *Excessive bail shall not be required, nor excessive fines imposed,* nor cruel and unusual punishments inflicted.

1. _____

V. No state shall without consent of Congress, *lay any imposts or duties on imports or exports,* except what may be absolutely necessary for executing its inspection laws; and the net produce of all exports, shall be for the use of the Treasury of the United States.

1. _____

VI. *The Congress shall have power to lay and collect taxes on incomes from whatever source derived,* without apportionment among the several states and *without regard to any census or enumeration.*

1. _____

2. _____

VII. *The right of the people to be secure in their persons, houses, papers, and effects, against unreasonable searches and seizures, shall not be violated,* and no warrants shall issue but upon probable cause, supported by oath or affirmation, and particularly describing the place to be searched and the person or things to be seized.

1. _____

Putting the Constitution to Work

Read the following situations and decide which branch of the federal government would handle the problem. Put E (executive), L (legislative) or J (judicial) on the line according to the governmental branch you have chosen.

1. The secretary of state has resigned due to ill health. Which branch will replace him or her? _____

2. The federal highway system is in need of repair and expansion. Which branch of the government will see to it that the money is available to accomplish this? _____

3. Opponents of a state law believe the law to be contrary to the United States Constitution. To which branch will they appeal? _____

4. A trade agreement is needed between the United States and a foreign nation. Which branch of the federal government will handle the situation? _____

5. New York and New Jersey are in dispute over a parcel of land. Which branch will handle the dispute? _____

Laws in Our World

All societies and groups govern themselves with certain rules to guide behavior and to protect their rights. Which rules of your school, home, and government protect your rights? (You may wish to check your student handbook.) List the rules that guide and protect you.

AT HOME

Example: Each member of the family agrees to limit telephone calls and to give each other privacy during those calls.

1.

2.

3.

4.

5.

IN SCHOOL

Example: Running in the halls is prohibited.
1.

2.

3.

4.

5.

OUR GOVERNMENT

Example: The federal government tests new food and drug products before they can be offered to the public.
1.

2.

3.

4.

5.

Create an Amendment

Amendments to the United States Constitution are made by the approval of two-thirds of the members of Congress. Amendments are made to update the Constitution to today's society.

What amendments would you like to see added to the United States Constitution? Remember, this will affect all Americans!

Let's Debate!

The Constitutional Convention was filled with debates and compromises. Listed on this page are some of the issues that were discussed and decided upon at that meeting. Select one or two issues to debate. Divide your group into two teams, each representing a different side of the issue. Carefully research the issue and use concrete facts to build up your argument. List some facts under each question to help you to prepare for the debate. Try to anticipate the other side of the argument.

1. Should we have a single leader or a group of leaders for our government? One group should represent the idea of having one President and the other the idea of having a body of equal leaders.

_____

_____

_____

2. Should each state have one vote or should each state be represented according to its population? One group should represent the larger states and the other the smaller states.

_____

_____

_____

3. Should we have a strong central government to make all the decisions? One group should represent the small farmers and the other the large landowners and big business.

_____

_____

_____

How did the Constitutional Convention settle each of these issues?

_____

_____

_____

_____

_____

_____

Create a Political Cartoon

Benjamin Franklin drew the political cartoon pictured at the left to illustrate the need for the colonies to unite. With this activity you, too, will be a political cartoonist! Select one of the main issues of the Constitutional Convention and create a political cartoon that will reveal your feelings about the issue. You may make your cartoon humorous by exaggerating details or by using satire.

Issue: _____

_____

_____

For Your Own Protection

Why is the Bill of Rights important to you as a citizen? List the ways your life might be different without the first ten amendments to the Constitution.

_____

_____

_____

_____

_____

_____

_____

_____

_____

_____

_____

_____

Draw a picture to illustrate one of the ways your life would be different.

Just Imagine

Imagine that you could travel back in time and attend the Constitutional Convention. Which people would you want to meet? What questions would you ask them?

People	*Questions*

Systems Check

The system of checks and balances keeps any one branch from becoming too powerful. Complete the chart to show how the system works.

This branch	*checks on this branch*	*in this way...*
Congress	President	
Congress	Supreme Court	
Congress	President	
Congress	Supreme Court	
President	Supreme Court	
President	Congress	
Supreme Court	President	
Supreme Court	Congress	

Constitutional Time Line

The following events were involved with the development of the United States Constitution. Put these events in order by numbering them from one to ten.

A _____ Annapolis Convention

B _____ Adoption of the Articles of Confederation

C _____ Battle of Trenton

D _____ Election of a president of the Constitutional Convention

E _____ Declaration of Independence

F _____ Ratification of the Constitution by nine states

G _____ First Continental Congress

H _____ Connecticut Compromise

I _____ Constitutional Convention called

J _____ Signing of the Constitution

More Critical- and Creative-Thinking Activities

1. Make a poster describing the weaknesses of the Articles of Confederation.

2. Compare and contrast the Articles of Confederation and the United States Constitution.

3. Memorize and recite the Preamble to the Constitution.

4. Paraphrase the Preamble of the Constitution in your own words.

5. Choose one of the original thirteen states. Find out if there were any unusual circumstances under which that state ratified the Constitution.

6. Write a clear summary of the work done at the Constitutional Convention.

7. Find out when your present state constitution was written.

8. Analyze why the United States Constitution has weathered the test of time.

9. Take the viewpoint of an Anti-Federalist. Prepare your opening and/or closing remarks for a debate.

10. Design a monument to honor the delegate you feel made the greatest contribution to the Constitutional Convention.

11. Read Article I: Section 7 of the Constitution and diagram how a bill becomes a law.

12. Read Article I: Section 8 of the Constitution and chart the eighteen powers delegated to Congress.

13. Read Article I: Section 9 of the Constitution and explain how the denial of these powers to the federal government protects the liberties of individuals.

14. Create a bulletin board display about the Bill of Rights.

15. Analyze how each of the first ten amendments affects your life. Which affects you most directly? Which affects you the least?

SECTION V:
Mock Convention

Constitutional Convention
Rules of Procedure

1. A member rising to speak must always address the president of the convention.

2. When a member is making a speech, other delegates are not to speak to each other or read books, pamphlets, or newspapers.

3. No member is to speak more than twice on the same question unless given special permission by the membership.

4. Any matter that is brought up on the floor of the convention may be brought up again and reconsidered.

5. Yea and nay votes do not have to be recorded because delegates are permitted to change their minds on an issue.

6. All proceedings of the Constitutional Convention are to remain secret until adjournment of the convention.

7. Representatives from seven states must be present for any vote. (quorum)

8. State roll call for voting starts with New Hampshire and proceeds with a southerly direction to Georgia.

These are the rules that were established at the Constitutional Convention in Philadelphia in 1787. Use them to guide you during your mock convention.

Choosing a Convention President

George Washington was unanimously chosen to be president of the Constitutional Convention. Use your research skills to investigate Washington's background and discover the leadership and personal qualities that inspired the trust and respect of the delegates. List as many factors as you can. An example is given.

1. George Washington gained leadership experience when he served as commander-in-chief of the colonial army.

_____

_____

_____

_____

_____

_____

_____

_____

_____

_____

_____

_____

_____

_____

_____

_____

Choose a student to play the role of George Washington at the mock convention. You might want to hold an election to decide.

Select a Delegate

What are the qualities that would enable a person to be a good delegate to represent a group at a meeting, conference or convention? List as many qualities as you can.

_____   _____
_____   _____
_____   _____
_____   _____
_____   _____
_____   _____
_____   _____
_____   _____

Everyone in the class will choose or be assigned a different delegate to represent. Be sure the most important delegates from all twelve states are represented.

The framers of the Constitution were all dedicated, intelligent, and politically wise. Many were multi-talented and served in a variety of professions. The Profiles Section of this book will help you make your decision. Use this page to gather facts about your delegate's personality, background, achievements, and political stand. **The more outside research you do, the better prepared you will be for the mock convention!**

Delegate: _____ *State:* _____

Facts About the Delegate: _____

_____
_____
_____
_____
_____
_____
_____
_____
_____

Get to Know Your State

As a delegate to the Constitutional Convention, you will have to be knowledgeable about many aspects of the state you represent. This will help you to have a better understanding of the state's point of view on the main issues of the convention. Use this page to help you research and organize information about your state.

State: _____

State's Population in 1787 Compared to Other States: _____

_____

State's Land Area in 1787 Compared to Other States: _____

_____

Main Industries: _____

_____

_____

Transportation and Exchange of Goods: _____

_____

Attitude toward Slavery: _____

_____

_____

State Politics: _____

_____

_____

Historical Facts: _____

_____

_____

_____

Loyalty to England: _____

Other Pertinent Information: _____

_____

_____

Learn the Issues

Below are listed one side of each of several issues that faced the delegates of the Constitutional Convention. After you have read each, decide how you, as the delegate you have chosen, would have reacted. Would you have been for or against each of these issues?

1. Each state should have the same number of representatives without regard to the population of the state.

2. The national government and its laws should have power and control over the individual states.

3. The executive office (President) should receive a salary.

4. Only landowners and the wealthy should be able to vote for members of the United States House of Representatives (Congress).

As _____, delegate of the state of _____,

I would be . . .

(in favor of/against) No. 1 for the following reasons:

_____

_____

_____

(in favor of/against) No. 2 for the following reasons:

_____

_____

_____

(in favor of/against) No. 3 for the following reasons:

_____

_____

_____

(in favor of/against) No. 4 for the following reasons:

_____

_____

_____

Classroom and Student Preparation

The following items should be considered options you may wish to incorporate into the presentation of a re-enactment of the Constitutional Convention. Each of these ideas may be limited or enhanced depending upon the depth of involvement you wish to pursue and the age and interest levels of your students.

Classroom

1. With magic markers and/or poster paint prepare a mural on craft paper to serve as background and to add atmosphere.

2. Student desks may be covered in dark green paper or fabric (such as dyed sheets) to resemble the baize-covered desks at which the delegates worked.

3. If possible, arrange the students' desks in semi-circular rows with the teacher desk (superior size) facing the student desks front and center.

4. Each student desk may have a name plate identifying it by state and delegate name. Group delegates from each state together.

5. Students may wish to create ''ink pots'' from aerosol spray caps or similar containers. If filled with pebbles, these will hold a pen upright.

6. Quill pens may be simulated in several ways.
   a. Attach real feathers to pens or pencils with glue or tape.
   b. Use the pattern provided in this section.
   c. Parent volunteers may assist in the manufacture of quill pens from feathers found locally.
   d. Some students may have facsimile quill pens from visits to historical gift shops.

Students

Students may wish to dress for the occasion.

1. Roll pant legs to knee length and wear knee-high socks.

2. Almost any shoe will look more authentic than athletic shoes.

3. Neck frills can be made by ruffling scraps of cloth or white crepe paper.

4. Tri-corn hats can be made of construction paper or oak tag.

General

Don't forget to give yourself and your students some well-deserved publicity.

1. Write a newsletter to parents.

2. Invite parents, other teachers, administrators, and other classes to the re-enactment.

3. If space is a problem, limit your invited guest list to superintendent, principal, board members, and/or parents.

4. Arrange for a photographer to cover the event. Perhaps a parent volunteer (you pay for film and developing) will take photos or videotape the event. You may want to ask the A.V. specialist for assistance.

5. Contact local daily and weekly newspapers. Send news releases in the time frame they suggest. Weekly ''shoppers'' frequently accept written articles for publication.

6. Contact local radio and television stations, both cable and commercial. You never know when they may have time to televise a spot report like this event.

7. Make a presentation of your photos, slides or video at a P.T.A., Board of Education, Mothers Club, Fathers Club, Jaycees, and/or other such meeting. Be sure to involve the students in the preparation and the presentation.

8. HAVE FUN!

A Delegate's Diary

As a delegate to the Constitutional Convention, most of your time is taken up by the demanding work of the meeting; however, in a diary entry you have the opportunity to describe the conditions of life that existed in Philadelphia during the summer of 1787. Include information about your lodgings, the type or clothing and wig that you wore, and the kind of food you ate and where you ate it. Describe the weather conditions and the activities of the city. You will need to research the information in order to present an accurate word picture.

Dear Diary,   Aug 1, 1787

Signed,

Quill Pen
Pattern

Trace the
pattern onto
heavy card stock.
Cut it out.

Cut out the
two small circles.
Insert a pen or pencil.

Constitutional Quiz

Fill in the blanks.

1. The first ten amendments are known as _____.

2. _____ is known as the Father of the Constitution.

3. Many Americans feared a strong central government because _____ _____.

4. _____ was a weakness of the Articles of Confederation.

5. _____ was another weakness of the Articles of Confederation.

6. "We the People" begins the _____ to the Constitution.

7. The _____ Compromise, or Great Compromise, decided state represention in Congress.

8. The system of checks and balances is important because _____.

9. The _____, passed under the Articles of Confederation, provided for the governing of new western lands.

10. _____ was the only state not to send delegates to the Constitutional Convention.

11. The first state to ratify the Constitution was _____.

12. The series of newspaper articles, written by Hamilton, Madison, and Jay in defense of the Constitution and urging ratification are called *The* _____ *Papers.*

Match each delegate with the appropriate description.

_____ 13. Signed the Declaration of Independence, Articles of Confederation, and Constitution   A. Benjamin Franklin

_____ 14. Virginian who refused to sign the Constitution   B. George Washington

_____ 15. Absent from the convention; U.S. Minister to France   C. James Madison

_____ 16. Recorded happenings at the convention; became fourth President   D. Alexander Hamilton

_____ 17. Eldest delegate at the Constitutional Convention   E. Gouverneur Morris

_____ 18. President of the convention; Virginia delegate   F. Thomas Jefferson

_____ 19. New York delegate; became first Secretary of the Treasury   G. George Mason

_____ 20. Draft of the Constitution is in his handwriting   H. Roger Sherman

Delegates to the Constitutional Convention and the Dates Ratified

Fifty-five delegates attended the Constitutional Convention. Thirty-nine delegates were present and signed the Constitution. Three delegates were present but did not sign the document; they were Elbridge Gerry, George Mason, and Edmund Randolph. The other thirteen were not present at the time of signing.

CONNECTICUT (January 9, 1788)
Oliver Ellsworth*
William Johnson
Roger Sherman

DELAWARE (December 7, 1787)
Richard Bassett
Gunning Bedford, Jr.
Jacob Broom
John Dickinson
George Read

GEORGIA (January 2, 1788)
Abraham Baldwin
William Few
William Houston*
William Pierce*

MARYLAND (April 16, 1788)
Daniel Carroll
Daniel of St. Thomas Jenifer
Luther Martin*
James McHenry
John Mercer*

MASSACHUSETTS (February 6, 1788)
Elbridge Gerry*
Nathaniel Gorham
Rufus King
Caleb Strong*

NEW HAMPSHIRE (June 21, 1788)
Nicholas Gilman
John Langdon

NEW JERSEY (December 18, 1787)
David Brearley
Jonathan Dayton
William C. Houston*
William Livingston
William Paterson

NEW YORK (June 26, 1788)
Alexander Hamilton
John Lansing*
Robert Yates*

NORTH CAROLINA (November 21, 1789)
William Blount
William Davie*
Alexander Martin*
Richard Spaight
Hugh Williamson

PENNSYLVANIA (December 12, 1787)
George Clymer
Thomas Fitzimons
Benjamin Franklin
Jared Ingersoll
Thomas Mifflin
Gouverneur Morris
Robert Morris
James Wilson

SOUTH CAROLINA (May 23, 1788)
Pierce Butler
Charles Cotesworth Pinckney
Charles Pinckney

VIRGINIA (June 25, 1788)
John Blair
James Madison
George Mason*
James McClurg*
Edmund Randolph*
George Washington
George Wythe*

Rhode Island ratified the Constitution on May 29, 1790.

*Delegates who did not sign the document

Suggested Resources

Young Readers

Commager, Henry. *The Great Constitution.* New York: Bobbs-Merrill, 1961

Cooke, Donald E. *America's Great Document: the Constitution.* New York: Hammond, Inc., 1959.

Findlay, Bruce and Esther. *Your Rugged Constitution.* Stanford, California: Stanford University Press, 1959.

Hayman, Le Roy. *The U.S. Constitution.* New York: Four Winds Co., 1970

Morris, Richard. *The First Book of the Constitution.* New York: Franklin Watts, 1976.

O'Reilly, Kevin. *Critical Thinking in U.S. History: Colonies to Constitution.* Pacific Grove, California: Critical Thinking Press, 1990.

Vaughan, Harold. *The Constitutional Convention—1787.* New York: Franklin Watts, 1976.

Wade, Linda. *James Madison.* Hawthorne, New Jersey: January Productions, Inc. 1993.

Adults

Bowen, Catherine Drinker. *Miracle at Philadelphia: The Story of the Constitutional Convention, May to September 1787.* Boston: Little, Brown, 1966.

Brant, Irving. *The Bill of Rights: Its Origin and Meaning.* Indianapolis: Bobbs-Merrill, 1965

Broderick, Francis. *The Origins of the Constitution: 1776-1789.* New York: Macmillan, 1964.

Levy, Leonard. *Essays on the Making of the Constitution.* New York: Oxford University Press, 1969.

Mc Gee, Dorothy. *Framers of the Constitution.* New York: Dodd, Mead, 1963

Morris, Richard. *Seven Who Shaped Our Destiny.* New York: Harper and Row, 1973.

Van Doren, Carl. *The Great Rehearsal: The Story of the Making and Ratifying of the Constitution of the U.S.* New York: Viking Press, 1948

Films

Birth of a Nation Video Series (VHS). Chatsworth, California: AIMS Media.

Cradle of Liberty (16mm). Philadelphia Trade and Convention Center.

The Constitution: The Compromise That Made A Nation (16mm). New York: Learning Corporation of America, 1975.

The Great Rights (cartoon). Brandon Films.

Independence: Philadelphia 1774-1800. (VHS). Huntsville, Texas: Educational Video Network.

Inventing a Nation: American Series (Alistair Cooke) 16mm.   New York: Time-Life.

The Living Constitution (16mm). Hollywood, California: Aims Media, 1976.

A More Perfect Union (VHS). Madison, Wisconsin: Knowledge Unlimited, 1991.

The U.S. Constitution Confronts the Test of Time (filmstrip/cassette). New York: Current Affairs, 1975.

MISCELLANEOUS

1787 Simulation Game. (Kit) Chicago, Illinois: Clearvue/EAV.